T0064985

the yelp

★ ★ ★ ★ ★

the yelp

★ ★ ★ ★ ★

A Heartbreak in Reviews

Chase Compton

Skyhorse Publishing

Copyright © 2016 by Chase Compton

All rights reserved. No part of this book may be reproduced in any manner without the express written consent of the publisher, except in the case of brief excerpts in critical reviews or articles. All inquiries should be addressed to Skyhorse Publishing, 307 West 36th Street, 11th Floor, New York, NY 10018.

Skyhorse Publishing books may be purchased in bulk at special discounts for sales promotion, corporate gifts, fund-raising, or educational purposes. Special editions can also be created to specifications. For details, contact the Special Sales Department, Skyhorse Publishing, 307 West 36th Street, 11th Floor, New York, NY 10018 or info@skyhorsepublishing.com.

Skyhorse® and Skyhorse Publishing® are registered trademarks of Skyhorse Publishing, Inc.®, a Delaware corporation.

Visit our website at www.skyhorsepublishing.com.

10 9 8 7 6 5 4 3 2 1

Library of Congress Cataloging-in-Publication Data is available on file.

Cover design by Laura Klynstra
Cover photo: iStockphoto

Print ISBN: 978-1-5107-1360-4
Ebook ISBN: 978-1-5107-1361-1

Printed in China

Contents

Prologue

THE CITY OF NEW YORK has been drenched in romantic mythology since the dawn of time. It is a place that has come to be known for its stories of love and longing and heartaches and heartbreaks lurking on every side street of the Village and beyond. As a teenager dreaming about New York, I thought about the great love stories that seemed to be a common occurrence on this enchanted island.

I believed in fiction and rationalized that all fiction must surely come from a place that actually exists. Woody Allen, Carrie Bradshaw, and other such feeble-hearted dreamers were the idols that I looked up to when I decided to come here. Their stories flashed out in black and white over sunsets and cinematic views of skylines from bridges I'd never set foot on. In the books I read and the films I watched, I plastered a vision of myself and my own heart on top of these stories that once belonged to someone else. I wanted to be a part of that vibrant, all-encompassing romance that seemed to drip from the pores of the natives on that island. I wanted Manhattan the way that the nerdiest girl in school looks at the captain of the cheerleading team: with unbridled longing. No matter that I'm a dude.

Romance and make-believe are often intertwined when it comes to love in New York City. We all, at one point or another, hope for that moment that steals your heart as you take Prince or Princess Charming by the hand and gaze out at the sunset over the Hudson. We come here believing in fairytales and love potions (which in modern times have come to be called "gin") and happily-ever-afters. For whatever reason, this place just made the fairytale seem so real. Those fireflies dancing in the bushes of Washington Square Park? I watched them with my eyes peeled, hoping for my own Jiminy Cricket to pop out. I watched and waited, praying that they were so much more than bugs blinking a bioluminescent booty call.

When I was eighteen years old, I ran away to Manhattan to see what all the fuss was about. Fresh out of high school and with only two hundred dollars to my name, I fled my small hometown in California. It seemed like the thing to do at the time. I had two choices: staying in the happy and sun-drenched hamlet of my youth, probably later going into art school in Los Angeles and growing up to be a fine West Hollywood delinquent, *or* jumping into something unknown and dangerous that had the ability to kill me. At the point in my young life where I was still discovering who I was and what I wanted, I was rather surprised to find out that I was more inclined to the latter.

New York opened her arms and took me in. This was probably the reason most kids like me sought her out: she just couldn't say no to wayward vagrants looking to lose themselves completely. So I dove in, and I tried to get to the bottom of what all of the poets and lovers and dreamers were fussing about. They say that "if you can make it here, you can make it anywhere."

I didn't realize that old saying didn't necessarily refer to love. I guess they were just talking about locking down a shitty little apartment and maybe a decent job that didn't make me want to kill myself. Love, it turns out, was a much more mysterious and elusive creature. Eventually, I was able to lock down an apartment in the depths of pre-gentrified Brooklyn and a few different jobs waiting tables, making coffee, and bartending all around the city. In my day-to-day, I still kept my eyes peeled for the one thing that was my real reason for coming to New York City:

Him.

I wasn't sure what he looked like or what kind of man he would be. I didn't know where I would find him: sitting at the old coffee shop where I spent most of my days off, writing poetry and chain smoking, trying to catch wayward glances of other mysterious-looking boys who might be the one. Would I have to go to a gay bar, armed with my fake ID and a smile, and pry open some complete stranger with vodka cranberries and my not-so-well-disguised California charm?

As a young New Yorker, I ended up finding several different gentleman callers to entertain my days. With an open mind and an open heart, I gave myself completely to these boys who I desperately hoped would fill that space in my heart I was saving for Mr. Right. There was the waiter I dated after I left him a poem on the bill for the burger I ate at some restaurant in Chelsea. He bought me a very pretty candle when I made my first journey into New Jersey to see him, and we lit it before we made love the first time. I don't remember why he and I never worked out, but it was inconsequential because shortly after him came the curly-haired opera singer who lived on Minetta Lane. Each time I went over to his apartment, I could only think of how badly I wanted to live on that street—it was surely the most beautiful street in all of Manhattan, and it was a block away from my favorite coffee shop! I still lived in the depths of Bushwick, where I, at one point, had to crawl over a dead cat that was covered in McDonalds cheeseburgers to get to my front door. Surely that kind of thing would never happen on Minetta Lane. Alas, eventually we broke up as well.

Looking back, I can recall each of the boys I had loved in my search for romance in the big city. I remembered the cab-driver-turned-photographer from Chicago; the club kid from Denver who, because he was born in Roswell, thought he was an alien; the yogi that I lived with for two years; and the boy from Los Angeles with the underwear-model-good-looks whom I took under my wing when times were tough for him. They all had their place in my heart at one point or another, but for whatever cosmic reason, none of them felt like the right fit. So I continued to grow older and wiser, learning from each new person I chose to let into my heart. I considered it all to be practice for the real love that was out there waiting.

It was here in Manhattan where I grew up into the man I am today. It was the search for true love amidst armies of aimless masses that turned me into the person that I was destined to be. With my eyes open and my arms wide, I carried on just as anyone else would have.

I worked my jobs, paid my bills, and paved a life for myself in the city of dreamers. Life went on just as I had expected it to until there came a point where it couldn't any longer. I didn't know it at the time, but I was about to embark on a journey that would be the catalyst for all of this mess—which would raise the stakes and scare the ever-loving shit out of me.

Introduction

Paris, 2013

AS I READIED MYSELF to leave, I knew I was dangling terrifyingly close to full-blown panic. It had been so easy last time I had fled to Paris on a whim—but those were different times, and I was a very different person. Maybe I was a child back then, and that was why I took to escaping with a child-like wonder and lust for the unknown. It was as if fleeing NYC had always been in the back of my mind.

Back then, all I wanted was to be a stranger again. I had grown weary of the same streets that I had known since I was a teenager. As complex and constantly changing as New York was, it was still all like second nature to me. I could close my eyes and navigate the winding streets of the Village as if I had an internal compass. As much as I hated to admit it, it was becoming evident that no matter how much you love something, it can spoil you in the end. Like a relationship gone cold, I had grown to recoil at New York's touch, her smell, her overall predictability.

Years ago, I thought that Paris would fill the gap in my heart that was a direct result of my complacency with Manhattan. Because I was not ready to let my love for Manhattan die, I attempted to breathe life into the city to whom I had pledged allegiance. Although it seemed counterintuitive, an affair was in order. I needed the touch of something new to rekindle the fire I once held so ardently, and it felt almost like a betrayal. So I rushed into another's arms to make sure that the one I had devoted myself to was in fact the one I was intended to be with.

My father had told me to go and find myself as if I hadn't a clue who I was in my relationship with the Big Apple. He was right, after all. So I went, and I soaked in the love and the romance of France. I let it envelop me, and it filled me like a tick to the point of bursting. It wasn't until I was lying flat on my back on the Champ de Mars that it all began to make sense. I was in love more so than I had ever been before. With New York. With the one I always knew I should be with.

She was a bitch. She got on my nerves, and there was absolutely zero subtlety in the daily struggle that was slowly hardening my once whimsical nature into a calloused drone. It was something I had heard from my peers who had lived in Manhattan for any amount of extended time—she *changed* you. The feeble were crushed by her, and the ambitious were fortified by the scar tissue that came with her wounds. Somehow, I was convinced that I was one of the ones that was made stronger by the adversity of the city. She made me a crazy person at times, but I always knew that she was the one. That was the first time I realized that love at first sight was not just the fodder of romantic comedy. When you meet the one, you just know.

Eventually it happened again—love at first sight. Five years passed, and I'd settled into my relationship with the City like an old married couple. It was comfortable, the way a marriage grows to be. There was often no need for words to fill the silences of our time together, and that had possibly stunted my budding literary ambitions. I had stopped writing love letters to New York only a few months after returning. I no longer had to woo her—I knew she was mine already. Clearly this was to become a problem, because without adversity, I knew I would never be capable of any necessary growth or change. That was why I was so swept off my feet the moment I met Him.

Out of nowhere came this *person*. He was the type of person I had always wanted to be with but never had the balls to actually pursue. He was not like all the ones before—he was different. I knew this upon our first meeting, and it made love at first sight feel like a real thing again. In a ragged tee shirt and saggy sweatpants, he had come to meet me one night for a drink. Perhaps this was why I knew that I loved Him—even at his worst I thought he was the most arrestingly stunning boy I had ever seen. The sweatpants be damned—I couldn't avert my gaze from that mouth. That smile! Those lips that I wanted to take into my own and swallow whole. He was beautiful.

Not only was he the most magnificent boy I had ever seen, but he was also utterly insane. I didn't know this right away, but within the next few days it began to show itself in subtle ways. He had a way of living life that left me so many times aghast—and quite honestly dumbfounded. Before I actually got to know Him, I found myself picking my jaw up off of the floor because of the things he would say.

He spoke in a language that I was immediately fluent in. More than that, often he didn't need words to convey what a knowing glance could—his eyes widened like a cartoon with one raised eyebrow, which denoted "are you seeing this shit?" He was hilarious. He was crazy. He was full of life and light.

This was immediately apparent to me the first time he took my hand while we walked through Washington Square Park. As his fingers intertwined with mine, they didn't clench but rather wrapped around mine playfully. His grasp was engaging, and it begged me to follow and dance with it. He was utterly boyish, and it was suddenly something that I realized I was insanely turned on by. It was if I was looking in a distorted funhouse mirror of myself before Paris. He was wide eyed with the intensity of springtime in New York City as he discovered it for the first time. It can be an overwhelming thing. Perhaps a little too overwhelming. Much like myself several years prior, he too was fresh off the plane from California.

Willingly, I threw myself into a whirlwind. I spent every waking moment drowning in the amazing feeling that he had resurrected in what I assumed was a plateauing ennui. Every street in SoHo was suddenly new as I looked through his eyes. It made me feel alive and relevant again. Overcome with such intense feeling for these new sights, it was easy to fall in love. I saw what he saw, and I believe that I really saw Him. Frankly, I was obsessed with what I saw. It was a beautiful person with an exposed soul, and an intense *joie de vivre* that often left me exhausted and spent. I wanted to do everything with Him. Every meal was the most delicious I had ever eaten, every walk through the park was a cinematic screenshot of a film whose happy ending I could see myself in. I knew what I was getting myself into.

Much like I had loved the City, he loved me. I was his New York City. Surrounded by constant rapture and earthly delight was only a means to an end that would ultimately require Paris. If he loved me as much as I had loved my city, then it was only a matter of time before the brilliant luster of it all became a familiar and soft glow, no more than a firefly's light. That's the problem with loving something so openly and truly, I was sad to realize.

He grew tired of things going his way, and it devastated Him. I was helpless because I could never say no to Him. I was a junkie for seeing Him happy because through his eyes was now how I looked at the world. I had never thought it possible before, but I discovered the meaning of too much of a good thing. I sat and watched Him recoil and withdraw, and I felt like I was wilting. The very wellspring of my new-found content had suddenly gone dry. Happiness was the dam I built, and happiness was the poison that got me in the end. If I do say so myself—what a way to go.

I resented and delighted in the fact that it had all come full circle. I was returning to Paris again in a week, this time not to fall in love but to find out how to make love go away and somehow manage to keep my heart intact.

As fate would have it, he told me he was in love with me a few days before I was about to return to Paris—this time for nothing more than a vacation to celebrate my birthday. Said he loved me, although it echoed hollowly against the recent memory of Him telling me he could never love me the way I loved Him. The way he had told me he still constantly craved the company of others and that he didn't believe that he was even capable of "truly" being with another person reverberated through me. Yet like many people do post-breakup, he kept me close. On standby. Just in case, it seemed, he didn't find another in my absence. The red flags should have been everywhere, but I chose to ignore them. They say that love is blind, and I believed this to be true. But I began to lose focus and ultimately lose sight of myself in the process.

The real kicker is almost too embarrassing to mention. It is one of those things that we only dare to think of discussing in our normal lives. It was the way we had met, the way we came together in this sick little microcosm of New York love affairs. It happened in a sphere not of this world. It happened . . . via Internet. Yes—it's true. Forgive me as I break whatever poetic notions you had about our history. He found me on the Internet. Cut and dry.

They call it OkCupid, as if Cupid's victims are ever really okay with matters of the heart. Not GoodCupid or FairCupid or JustCupid. Just okay. Like Cupid has nothing better to do than just be tolerant of the tomfoolery that has occurred in his name. It seemed so innocent at the time, and I had merely sent Him a message saying that I loved the fact that he couldn't live without kale or drop-crotch pants. He was adorable—at least in pictures—and he sounded like he could be my kind of guy. So I did what I was supposed to do, and I told Him that I wanted to meet Him. That was the entire reason for me lurking through cyberspace on a goddamn dating website in the first place—to find someone. And for a moment, it seemed as if I had actually found someone.

Weeks later, after the whole affair was well on its course, I found time to steal away by myself to sit at the Champ de Mars. It was my thirty-first birthday. In the shadow of *la Tour Eiffel* I must have looked utterly typical, swathed in all-black garb and hiding my gaze behind dark sunglasses. Part of me expected to be angry, but I was not. It would seem impossible to be angry when basking in the Parisian ebb and flow of life, which was noticeably slow considering it was the slow season locally. It was familiar, and although it was the same Paris I had fled to years prior as a wanderlusting twenty-something, it seemed changed. Paris had emptied out, and all of the people had gone to the country or Provence for their vacations. The streets were oddly bare and at times frightfully silent. *Just perfect,* I thought to myself. *Perfect timing.*

I knew he was going to leave me for good eventually, despite all of these dramatic eleventh-hour breakups that never quite seemed to stick. I knew that all that I had come to adore was too good to be true. I could tell that it was going to happen even before I left. It had made the sting even more painful. It was not Him leaving me that hurt the worst, but that he had really and truly wanted me a matter of days before. As he lay asleep in my arms on that beautiful day on the pier, I held Him close to my chest as if he would suddenly wake and sprint away. I kissed his forehead as he slept and prayed that it could stay like this. Just for a little longer. I knew as it was happening that I wanted Him to stay.

He had told me over and over again that he could never be with me, and I had not believed Him. I thought surely something so perfect and so rare would not be crushed beneath the weight of . . . nothing. In truth, there was nothing wrong with the way things were progressing. It was just us being us. Me wanting too much, Him wanting too little—the classic relationship that was built to be razed. I couldn't have imagined it any other way, and it seemed that things were happening almost as if predicted by prophecy.

My life is a fucking tragic comedy, I thought to myself. I began to laugh as I cried. It was hilarious. I never thought I would be crushed so deeply while basking in the shade of the Eiffel Tower. Heartbroken in Paris. I laughed more, which only caused me to cry harder. By continuing to laugh at how much my life sucked, I hoped to distract any passersby from the tears that were falling from beneath my fake Ray Bans—I looked so fucking cool.

I had initially believed that Paris was the capital of romance, and that my whimsical heart would find comfort in her arms. I believed that the crows the size of cats that haunted every park were simply laughing and not as threatening as they appeared. But I had to convince myself it was all a movie set. The façade of romance was not real life. The crows weren't laughing—they were ugly and sinister. Paris would not make a romantic of me. Heartbreak was the new black in Paris, and I decided that if I must, I was going to rock it.

He would have left me in New York anyhow. I felt that maybe he had never truly wanted me in the first place. It was all a fluke, just another one of those strange and beautiful things that happens in the summer when the mind becomes too clouded with humidity and lust. I wished that he could only have had the courtesy to destroy me within the comfort of Lady Liberty. I wished that I could have finished writing my first novel in Montmartre while sipping a cappuccino instead of writing sad emails of resignation.

Most of all, I wished that he hadn't been so perfect. I wished that he hadn't come into my life and filled me with inspiration. If I knew that my ambition would have come at the price of my heart, I would have never accepted it. I would have turned, walked away, and went on with my sad and pathetic life of doing nothing but drinking myself to death and waiting tables. He had made me crave more—a happy life with love and peace and direction.

I had loved Him. I loved every crazy thing he did, even when it pissed me off. When he told me to slow down, I loved Him even more, because in my head, this meant that he actually wanted to be with me for the long haul. Ha.

So I sat there with the crows, and I smoked my delicious Lucky Strike Lights on the Champ de Mars and realized that I had to quit them upon my return. I had to savor every last drop of this moment frozen in time. I would never have my heart broken this hard again in Paris. I would never return here. I would never smoke these filthy cigarettes again if I wanted to prove to myself that I could move on. Never again would I be crying over a love that was so beautiful but so unattainable with the tears staining my black Helmut Lang shirt. I was killing it—I really was. This season's looks on all of the Paris runways would be Crushing Despair. Haute Heartbreak. Devastation Couture.

Heartbroken in Paris was the beginning of a real love story that I would one day write. I knew it could only get better from there. I was lower than I had ever been in my entire life, a sunken shell of my former adventuresome self. I would carry this with me for the rest of my life, always remembering the time when I started to take care of myself again. I would return to New York broken, a homeless vagabond in need of a new direction. I would write the next chapter of my life through different eyes.

How I wished that I could have taken Him with me. But then again, he was the catalyst for it all in the first place.

I hated it when stories had unhappy endings, so I decided to not let the story end. This chapter sure sucked, and I hated it, and I had never felt so lost and alone in my entire life, but I knew that there was still an epilogue to be had. That's the funny part about all of this mess—I already knew how it all would end. And it broke my heart.

Chapter One

I LAY ON THE FLOOR AND STARED at the ceiling. It was cold in my room, and I was only wearing one sock. I wasn't exactly sure how this had happened, but then again, I wasn't exactly sure if I cared. Outside, snow was coming down in buckets. It had been like this for weeks now, and much to my dismay, it showed no sign of stopping. I rolled onto my stomach and pressed my forehead to the cold wooden floor.

This wasn't the first time we had broken up. This was months after I returned from Paris, where he "officially" broke up with me over an email on my birthday. Heartbreak is a place we've all been to; I knew I wasn't special or anything. This was just a thing that happened. People's hearts get broken, and everyone feels like it has never happened to anyone else before in history like it is happening to them in that moment. But for a second I selfishly slipped and let myself believe that no Capulet nor Montague had ever felt the anguish that I now had pressing down on my chest. The devastation of the ages was now my best friend, and it felt like New York City was the perfect place to be if I wanted to wither away into a tiny ball of heartbreak and depression. I was the mayor of

Heartbreak. I was the crown prince of Despair. I owned it, and I wore it like a straightjacket.

What a drama queen.

I had just returned to the arctic tundra once known as Manhattan after an unexpected trip to California. I had escaped the East Coast two days after Thanksgiving, and for that I was thankful. I can say, without hesitation, that Thanksgiving 2013 was the worst day of my entire life. On a day that was supposed to be about family and friends and (most importantly) binge eating turkey, I had found myself curled up in fetal position on my couch, sobbing hysterically and unable to move. I was completely paralyzed, and the only thing I could do was cry. It didn't help that every half hour or so I would get festive text messages and pictures of grandiose dinner tables with little blurbs saying things like "Happy Thanksgiving! Wish you were here! So much turkey!"

Meanwhile, I craved a swift and painless death. I would gobble-gobble alright . . . a fistful of Valium, if I didn't know any better.

And I did know better, most of the time, but I just dug the hole even deeper. I met up with Him (who shall forever remain nameless) and tried to figure out what was going on. The thing is, I knew what was going on: our relationship was coming to an ugly end. He had betrayed me and shattered my trust, and there was nothing that was going to change that. A matter of days prior, we still had the intentions of moving in together and starting what I had hoped would be a "real adult relationship."

I had so many feelings and so few places to put them anymore. It boiled over in me like a pot simmering too high, and every once in a while it would get the best of me and completely incapacitate me. I felt wretched and sad and completely defeated. I thought long and hard about what had happened to me and tried to think of a way to fix the entire situation. Naturally, there was only one thing I could think to do that would make the feelings any less pungent.

I began to write letters to Him every morning when I awoke from my fitful slumber. I'd crawl out of bed looking like the Crypt Keeper and sulk my way over to my laptop by the couch. For minutes, I'd sit there and stare at the screen, wondering what I could say that would make any of this cruel plot twist any different. It wasn't so much about begging and pleading for Him to reconsider his sadistic actions and come back to me, but more about trying to get Him to remember all of the good stuff that he threw away when he decided that I wasn't enough. The letters I wrote Him were long and detailed, usually reminiscing about how happy we were together as we walked through the Village hand in hand on our way to breakfast or lunch. After I'd finish a letter I would sign it always the same way:

I love you. And I miss you.

Then I'd delete the entire thing.

The entire time we knew each other, he was constantly trying to escape. Then he'd come crawling back once he had successfully fled. Men in Manhattan were so typical at times, and I'd known them all. He had cut me loose—on my birthday—when I went to Paris. I received an email from Him telling me to drown in the Seine. Upon return, he had sought me out again and asked for forgiveness, which

I was happy to extend. Weeks went by, and we had resumed our role as the happiest couple in all of New York, but eventually he came to meltdown again. It happened on Thanksgiving. I knew it would never be the same after that.

People deal with heartbreak in a myriad of different ways, but most of the time they are just a variation on the same general idea. The monologue by Julie Delpy from the last scene in the film "2 Days in Paris" came to mind, where Julie calmly states:

> Always the same for me: Break up, break down. Drink up, fool around. Meet one guy, then another, fuck around. Forget the one and only. Then after a few months of total emptiness start again to look for true love, desperately look everywhere. And after two years of loneliness, meet a new love and swear it is the one, until that one is gone as well.

Ouch.

I wondered if it was happening again, just as it always had. I'd been in love a few times before, and I honestly felt that I had a pretty firm grasp on what all that business was about. Stars get in your eyes, and every song is about *them*. Eyes lock during sex for a change, and you honestly see the person instead of just looking at them. You remember that suns set, and you notice them as if they are suddenly filled with meaning—even though they've been there, silent and unnoticed, all along. All of these were the things I had come to know about the nature of love, but for some reason this one felt different. I wondered if I thought this way about each new love at first, and then upon ending those trysts, erased that general knowledge like a dry-erase board crammed with fruitless equations.

If it all sounds very grim, that is not the intention. I am a rational man with a strong head on his shoulders, and I wouldn't have stuck around if my entire relationship with Him was a never-ending nightmare of deceit, lies, and sadness. That wasn't the way it always was, and to fully explain why I loved Him so dearly, one must know that to be the truth. As much as I had wanted to spread the gospel of what an evil monster he was, it would not be the full story. Being with Him made me the happiest person I'd ever been in my entire life.

Before Him, I always thought that the things I wanted out of life were "corny." At thirty years of age, I used to sit in the park and long for the storybook love that one usually only read about in a sixteen-year-old girl's diary. I wanted sunsets and sunrises on the beach, embracing each other curled up in an abandoned lifeguard tower. I wanted trips to get ice cream in the dead of winter, in the middle of the night, and sharing said ice cream with one spoon. I wanted a man to take my last name and sleep in bed with me in my parent's home back in California when we took vacations there. I was dog-crazy, even though I'd previously never even wanted one to call my own. Suddenly, every time a cute little Italian Greyhound pranced by me on the street, I nearly dropped to my knees with a swoon as I imagined what it would be like to own a dog with my partner.

I'd always been "that way." It was as if finding my soulmate was the most important thing in the world to me. Most gay men my age had different drives. Most of my peers made the gym their soulmate

(I both envied and despised the lousy fucks) or made a career their life's calling. People in the city were married to their work and to their futures. Sure—I had a job and paid my bills and took decent care of myself, but taking care of myself wasn't enough for me. I wanted with all my heart to find someone who I could take care of and who would in turn take care of me and perhaps propel me into . . . I don't know. Adulthood? Happiness? Wholeness?

If you've ever lived in Manhattan, you'll know what it is like to be the loneliest person in the entire world even when you are surrounded by millions of people: screaming cab drivers, ranting hobos, fighting children, chanting Hare Krishnas, clucking queens on 8th Avenue, growling punks on St. Mark's Place. There's always an ambulance, street performers, psychics, fanatics, and people, people everywhere. It's maddening to feel like, in the midst of all of the buzz, there isn't a single person on your team.

When I first met Him, I felt like I had finally found a teammate. He was a needle in a gaystack, everything I had ever wanted and more. He lived in Manhattan on the very same street I did, just across the length of the island. It was a straight shot from the West Village to the East on 4th, and I convinced myself that surely this must have been fate. He wore the same clothes as me—that sort of disheveled chic that was so au courant and involved a lot of black blousy things and painted on skinny jeans that we'd bought from Oak. He even had a job, too. Much like myself, he was a waiter. This made me feel better about life in general because I felt like he was in the same boat that I was in: trying to stay afloat while trying to pursue dreams by serving the masses. I was a failed artist and a would-be writer, and he was interested in pursuing a career in fashion. I could imagine the beautiful day when my fashion mogul boyfriend would attend my book signings draped in exquisite Rick Owens and smiling at me because we no longer had to wear aprons or ask anyone ever again "how would you like that cooked?"

And the sex? Forget about it.

He knew what he was doing. He held out for a month when we first started dating. Although we were attached at the lips and getting off every other way we could manage, he didn't actually fully give up the goods until I was completely enraptured with Him as a person. After we made love that first time, we couldn't stop. We fucked every day, sometimes twice or three times. It would be easy for me to say that I was obsessed with his physical beauty and sexual prowess, but that wasn't the case in the slightest. When he lay before me naked, sometimes I would just stare at Him, unable to move. His body was the most gorgeous I'd ever had the pleasure of seeing. Sure, I'd dated a muscle queen or two in my day, and one of my last loves had the body of a Greek god. His wasn't like that—it was the little things that turned me on with a passion I'd never known before. Besides his rippling muscles and his perfect ass, he was littered with imperfections. These were my favorite parts.

His feet were disgusting dinosaur claws with big chunks of blister peeling off of the heels. A scar from a hernia ran across his stomach. He had scars on his back from minor surgery to remove what could have become cancer, and his balls . . . his balls were a nightmare. He never trimmed his pubes, and it was a jungle down there. The talons, the scars, the jungle balls—these were my favorite things. His imperfections showed me that he wasn't the kind of guy you saw photoshopped to hell in a magazine or filtered out in the shimmery studio light of a porno set. He was real. He had lived. And his realness made Him the most extraordinary thing I'd ever been with.

I could wax poetic about how perfect he was to me for days. But that wouldn't change anything, and I had to find that out the hard way, because that was exactly what I did after Thanksgiving when everything fell apart. I waxed. Hard.

Chapter Two

THE CITY THAT WAS ONCE THE SCENE for what I considered to be my dream come true soon became my nightmare. On every street corner, I saw phantom images of the two of us in full swoon, dancing hand in hand. Every cup of coffee I attempted to take in was a war zone flashback set directly in the trenches that jolted me from my momentary reverie and sent me scurrying like a frightened animal. I must have looked positively feral as I darted in and out of every single café or restaurant in the West Village just trying to find myself breakfast. As a result of this, I quickly became very skinny. I'd always been a thin man, but this new inability to eat made me positively gaunt.

Because I couldn't eat, food of course became the one thing I wanted the most. Eating was what we had done best together in our short time. He was a big boy with a big appetite, and he always wore a smile from ear to ear when presented with a delicious meal. Because he spent time in the military, he ate like a wild animal. Watching him eat a pastrami sandwich was like watching the Tazmanian Devil whirl into a frenzy of swirling fury. It was insane. I loved it. No tablecloth was safe from Him, and by the end of a meal he always left the table looking like a battlefield.

I was sinking into a morbid depression and wasting away, and I didn't know what to do about it. I couldn't talk to my friends about it because they were sick and tired of the same old sob story. They all told me the same thing, anyhow: "He warned you he didn't want to be in a relationship. You did this to yourself." It pissed me off to no end.

"How can you not see that we conquered that?" I'd yell in retort. "We fixed it! He fell in love with me! He got a tattoo for me on his arm! He told me he wanted to move in, and start our lives together! Coney Island . . . Montauk . . . Central Park . . . The Temperance Fountain . . . All of those delicious dinners holding hands and staring into each other's eyes for hours . . ."

They would shake their heads and tell me I had imagined it all. This, also, infuriated me to no end, as I was convinced they hadn't a clue what was really going on. I wished that they could have seen the way he looked at me as we lay on top of each other everywhere we could possibly recline in Manhattan and beyond. I wished I could show them the way we used to laugh and eat and make love and (quite literally) skip through the streets of SoHo together.

I wanted to show everyone that it was indeed love, and it had happened, and it meant the world to me. And it was still happening—everywhere I turned, memories of Him. A war zone. A minefield of memories.

I sat in my underwear, shivering and manic. I needed to find a way to let Him, and the world at large, know that this love was not an illusion.

It was real as shit. It had rocked me. How did everyone not know that I had found my soulmate? How did magazines and newspapers and Barbara Walters not want to interview us about how we managed to find The Greatest Love of All Time? I felt like we deserved a medal or a trophy for how perfect and beautiful our happiness was. How did he not cherish this romance the same way I did? It was everything. I was there. I saw it. I lived it.

I had to get it out, so I did the only thing that I knew how to do. I wrote it.

I'd always written in my life, but for the first time ever I felt like nonfiction was more unbelievable than the greatest of love stories. Eat your heart out, Juliet. My man's twice the lover than that Montague dump of yours—and mine's actually *real*. He was flesh and blood, and he lived on this island with me, and we ate sandwiches together and did it in the butt.

I began to write the story of the rise and fall of the love of my life. I assumed that I would send it to Him one day in a beautifully bound book, and he would then realize that he had thrown away the greatest love he'd ever known. That was the plan. Or, of course . . . I could Facebook it. I could share our story with the whole world in the click of a button. Maybe if all of my friends and his friends and our mutual friends knew about our love, then it would be validated and real and he would come back to me.

I immediately knew that was crazy and stalker-ish and immature and totally wrong. If he didn't want to be with me, then that was his choice. All of our friends didn't need to know that something born of such love dissolved into such a mess. At the same time, I wanted someone to tell me that I was right. I wanted someone to tell me that it was love, and that it was real. I needed to get it out there into the world, and hopefully the world would understand me and the sad, blathering fool I had become.

I could retrace every single step of our relationship. Manhattan had become a map of memories, and every single bar and restaurant and park had become like a pin drop on it. Our story had happened in 3D, and the stage we had played it on was this great big island filled with millions of other people's "pins." I had to take a moment to force myself to understand that this same thing was probably happening to every other heartbroken weirdo in this city. I wished that there were a meeting place, like AA, where all of the heartbroken masses could congregate and hide away from those dreadful pins. I wondered if I could go someplace and just be listened to.

I don't know how it struck me initially, but I pulled up my laptop and began to write. Hungry as shit and in a frenzied fit of desperation, I could only think about eating at my favorite restaurant that I used to go to with Him. It was Café Mogador, in the East Village. I didn't know what to write, and I didn't know what to feel, but I began to write my story starting with where it was the happiest: breakfast.

It was that day that I wrote my first review on Yelp.

I'd known what Yelp was for years, and I had always hated it with a fiery passion. It was a waiter's worst nightmare. I remembered how my old boss used to read Yelp reviews daily and bring the spite and vitriol of the world into shift meetings every night before service.

"So this woman said her waiter wasn't nice to her and forgot to bring her ketchup when she asked for it. If you can't even bring ketchup to someone who asks for it, then you don't deserve a job here," my boss would say.

I'd sit there in pre-shift and shake my head, remembering exactly who the woman was who had written the ketchup review. She was a bitch. And her child spilled a soda on my shoes. And now she is exacting her *bitchy* revenge by being an anonymous *bitch* on Yelp, and it was ruining my shift. The Yelpers were my enemy, and I loathed their self-entitled bullshit.

Yelp was full of critics, and I found criticism to be often . . . well, mean. People were always so quick to say everything that they didn't like about a restaurant or bar, and those were the reviews that always got the most attention. No one ever got a raise for that Yelp about how the waiter brought a fork when they dropped theirs on the ground. It was a forum for whiny little brats with no voice in the world and people who needed validation. When people didn't have anyone to talk to in their "real" lives, then they could just bitch and moan into cyberspace and have other bitchers and moaners bitch and moan with them. And I thought to myself . . .

Fuck. That sounds delightful.

Yelp: the sound a wounded animal makes.

Café Mogador

☆ ☆ ☆ ☆ ☆

Category: Moroccan

Neighborhoods: East Village, Alphabet City

You may wonder how it is even possible that a man of thirty-one years of age has never eaten an egg. It's just the strangest thing, and I know I'm not normal. Everyone eats eggs. Me—I'm just all sorts of terrified.

I can't really explain it. They just always grossed me out. The first thing people always ask is, "Well, you've eaten cake before, right? That has eggs in it, you know." In truth, yes, I do know. I know that there are eggs in cake. Eggs are in everything, and if I didn't eat things with eggs *in* them, then I would surely starve to death. I'm not afraid of cake or mayonnaise or any sort of baked good, really. Just the egg itself in its natural form. Just like anything else in life, if it masquerades itself around in some unnoticeable vessel then I can happily stomach it. Tricking myself into things that I know disgust me has always been my forte as I am a classically trained masochist.

Brunch has always been a nightmare for me. There's never anything I want, and I often feel as if I'm letting everyone around me down. No, I do not want to share an eggs benedict with you. No, I do not want the burger every Saturday because it is the only thing on the menu that isn't topped with a big white-and-yellow skull and crossbones. I'll just have a mimosa, and sit there glaring at you (starving all the while) as you inhale your omelet and bitch about your boyfriend. I was never really a morning person to begin with, so this just adds fuel to the fire. Don't invite me to brunch. You'll hate me. I will single-handedly ruin your *huevos rancheros.*

Café Mogador was "our place." It was the scene of some of the best breakfasts of my entire life. Being madly in love, I would sit on the patio (which seems to be perpetually situated in springtime) and stare longingly into his eyes, wishing to fall into them like an endless cup of dark brown coffee. We were that couple. It's kind of gross, I'll admit to it. And have you ever seen someone try to use a knife and fork while holding someone's hand? It's like a one-handed clap, and it's really kind of hard to get anything done. Ever since I first met Him, I knew that I would forever live on the patio of Café Mogador with Him. Days I'm not there, I picture my table going completely unseated. Surely my ghost haunts it, hand in hand with his ghost, eating ghost merguez as fast as we can.

Every waitress at the Café is the nicest girl in the world, and the type of girl I would want to date if I were heterosexually inclined. They're all the type of girl you would want to take home to meet your mom and dad. You know who this waitress is: the epitome of the East Village waitress, who wears sweaters year-round and is always in a delightful mood and seems genuinely happy to bring you more hot sauce. It's good vibes, and it's like a drug to me—that sense of calm and joy that a good meal with good company can provide.

He's my favorite dining companion because everything tastes good when I'm around Him. He gets the Mediterranean eggs, and I get the halloumi eggs with a side of merguez—every time. It just feels right, and it feels like home, and it's what I always want. He reaches over the table without asking and removes the two eggs from my plate and places them on his own. Happily, I eat my halloumi eggs without eggs, which is essentially a pizza if you really think about it: za'atar pita, halloumi cheese, and roasted tomatoes.

Apparently I can do brunch without eggs. He takes care of it. And apparently I'm becoming a morning person, too. There is nothing in the world I would rather do than sit there on that patio and not eat eggs with Him.

Von

☆ ☆ ☆ ☆ ☆

Categories: Dance Clubs, Dive Bars
Neighborhood: NoHo

I suppose that to truly understand the story of Him, you have to begin at the beginning. I know it's repetitive, but it's the honest truth. The beginning is always the best part of a love story because that's where there's still hope. Everything is possible, and the plot twist hasn't happened yet. There's not even all the good stuff that comes along with love to exalt yet. It's just a meeting of two strangers in the world who have found each other and, through hope, start to build something that, hopefully, will change their lives.

In a city like this one, it's amazing anyone ever finds each other. There are so many of those theoretical fish swimming in this decadent, dirty sea. How does one begin to cast out their line and hope to catch a big one? How do you know when you meet The One?

I had only seen pictures of Him. I'd found Him in the swirl of cyberspace, and all I knew was that he was beautiful, funny, and we had things in common. Things we couldn't live without: kale and drop-crotch pants. That was all it took to get my attention—and the pixelated smile that jumped out from my laptop and begged, "Smile with me. I'm happy."

I asked Him to meet me on the first day of our contacting each other. At the time, we were both waiters who worked at restaurants in the same neighborhood. We were both getting done with work at the same time, and I suggested a drink at my local after-work watering hole, Von. For some reason, I just knew that I had to meet Him. Through an ongoing text message string that had lasted all evening long, I could surmise that he was the kind of person I wanted to surround myself with. That and that goddamn smile. Those dimples that looked like the largest of crescent moons just stuck there beneath his perfect cheekbones. I looked at the picture he had provided of himself on the website and felt as if I already knew Him.

He walked north on Lafayette. I walked south. On the corner of Bond Street, we met face to face for the first time. I immediately understood why he was so hesitant to meet me on this very day: he looked like hell. Not planning on going on a date this particular evening, he had basically worn pajamas to work. And it was perfect.

Normally, I would fuss and preen for the perfect first date. And I went on a lot of dates. I would wear the perfect costume and make a reservation at Indochine and have a nice bottle of wine already picked out. Not this time. For whatever reason, I felt immediately comfortable around Him. We sat in the back corner of Von and spoke of San Francisco and Fernet Branca and shopping at Oak. It was simple. It was easy. I immediately knew that I wanted this man to be my best friend. But more than that, I wanted to swallow

Him whole. I wanted to take Him into my mouth, taste Him, chew on Him, and revel in his being. I wanted Him on my skin like a sexual photosynthesis; I wanted to absorb Him. As he spoke effortlessly to me about his life, I couldn't stop staring at his lips. They moved in slow motion and at times the words seemed to not make any sense at all. He could have been speaking Swahili for all I knew. I just wanted to kiss Him.

Sometimes it's the kisses that I think about the most. I can remember what it was like on that first night when we kissed on Saint Mark's Place in front of Yaffa Café. My eyes were closed, but I could feel with my lips that his lips were smiling as they met mine. I'd kissed a lot of men in my days (see: sexually liberated, not a slut) and always thought that I knew what it meant when they referenced "fireworks." With Him, it wasn't fireworks. It was the mushroom cloud of an atomic bomb. It was Pompeii, fireflies, Christmastime, the feeling you get on the first day of spring.

At Von that first night, I leaned against the bar and was caught in a wave of unimaginable delight. He was perfect. Looking back, I suppose I can see how I thought that. I didn't know that he was the type of person that had the capacity to completely throw away another person's heart. If it sounds melodramatic, that's because it is. The heart is a funny thing, and it can make mountains out of molehills. Back then it was all so simple, and I was just a boy looking at another boy and seeing something that words could not yet explain. It was that unspeakable hope. Hope that this was The One, and I was finally getting back what I deserved from the universe.

The tragedy of it all is that I had to learn that the Devil comes dressed as your wildest dreams. Mine blinded me to the truth, and the truth is that in order to really be in love, it requires two hearts. One simply will not do. Even if it is the biggest, most pure and loyal heart there is.

The Coffee Bean & Tea Leaf
☆ ☆ ☆ ☆ ☆

Category: Coffee & Tea
Neighborhood: Greenwich Village

Ritual has been a vital part of the core of my being for as long as I can remember. In an almost compulsive fashion, I have taken to the things that have made me happy with a fervor that most associate with religious fanatics. If I see or do something that I like, I treat it like a sapling that needs tending, watering, and feeding until it blooms. As a young New Yorker and an artist, my rituals have been fairly simple. Most of the time, it involves just getting a morning cup of coffee and having a cigarette. Sure, it goes deeper, like my traditional gin martini with a twist that I must drink every Valentine's Day. Coffee, however, has always been the most prevalent.

In my life with Him, we used to go to the Coffee Bean & Tea Leaf every morning. It was one of those unspoken things that we just did every morning to help recover from the night before. For a while we switched to decaf because he began to have severe mood swings, which I usually took the brunt of. Little did I know at the time it wasn't the coffee's fault at all. Hindsight is 20/20.

In the very beginning of our courtship, we drank a lot. It was that sort of rose-colored fog of Cupid breath that winds one up into having to deal with hangovers of all sorts. Every barroom was painted red with the bitterness of Campari from his Negronis and the vibrancy of our newfound contentment. Dancing in the roads hand in hand, kissing beneath streetlights on Greenwich, kissing while rolling on the dirty sidewalks of Minetta Lane—we were a sight to behold. I was drunk on love and on Him and on gin—and it didn't matter at all. I knew that the morning would come eventually, and I would wake up with Him in my arms. Then he'd roll over and stare at me. Without thinking, I would get up and throw on whatever clothes were on the floor so that I could go get us coffee. It was always me that ran downstairs to the Coffee Bean for coffee. I was just as hung over and decimated as he, but it brought me insane joy to go do this little ritual for Him.

Those days, I didn't see many other people. So many of my personal relationships were put on hold so that I could spend every waking moment with what I knew was the man of my dreams. It didn't bother me in the slightest because he had become my best friend. The Bonnie to my Clyde. The Ethel to my Lucy. The Campari to my gin. At last it all made sense. My mother had always told me that when I met "the one," I would just know. As far as I knew, he was it. Looking back, perhaps I was just drunk. Or had too much coffee.

The baristas of the Coffee Bean & Tea Leaf became the most regular reoccurring characters in my life. My ritual of seeing them every morning became the best part of my day. With a smile, they would serve me my two coffees with a knowing look on their faces. I could tell that they could tell that I was stupid in love. At times, they would give me the once-over, as if they knew that I was dripping with morning love making and looking like a disheveled mess. Cockeyed and wearing crumpled floor-clothing, I would just give them a Cheshire-cat grin as I waited for freshly brewed light roast.

Then there were the days when he would come and get coffee with me before we went on our morning walks. He'd cling to my arm so tight, like he was afraid I'd float away if he didn't hold me close enough. Then the baristas would smile at us because we were finally becoming "regulars."

Being a regular was all I ever wanted. As someone who came to New York City at a very early age, I had been trying to find a "place" my entire young life. As rituals tend to go, if you do something enough times and it feels good, then you become regular. It's what you do. I thought the same would always hold true with me and Him. I made Him my ritual, and over black coffee and hangovers, I painted a picture of what I wanted my life with Him to be like. It was the happiest I had ever been, and it felt so good to finally be a regular.

Uncle Ted's Modern Chinese Cuisine

☆ ☆ ☆ ☆ ☆

Category: Chinese
Neighborhood: Greenwich Village

Uncle Ted's makes me want to be a better person.

Wait—let me rephrase that. I want to be a better person, and Uncle Ted's is to blame. No, still not right. Damn. When I think about what a sad person I used to be, I can only hearken back to a time when Uncle Ted's was there for me as the ultimate cliché comfort. Yeah, that's more like it.

Chinese food always reminds me of being in love. It's that age-old classic image of being completely involved with someone so romantically that you don't mind letting them see you gorge on lo mein and General Tso's chicken like an utter pig. It usually happens in sweat pants after a hard day's work and is a lesson in just existing with another person and your carbs. It is eaten out of the paper to-go box that we all know and love, and it feels like it would be best enjoyed if eaten off an upturned cardboard box used as a makeshift table. Words cease to matter in that moment that you first begin to savor your eggroll. That's just the way of it. You know the feeling.

I remembered the day I did "the purge." We had been planning it all week, and he was dead-set on doing a full-blown overhaul of my disgusting apartment. Don't get me wrong, I'm not a disgusting person. All of my things are placed carefully in their rightful places. However, there was clutter and dust that was so artfully hidden that one would never notice it until they got on their hands and knees or (God forbid) looked under the bed.

Just beneath the surface of my slumber, tucked haphazardly away, were at least a dozen paintings I had done that would never see the light of day. Some pieces were unfinished and would stay that way for eternity, and others were just plain hideous and born from a very strange abstract period that I went through both literally and emotionally. It would be a full day's worth of work to eradicate all of the dust, scrub all of the corners, and get rid of all my pointless paintings that were hidden away.

We scoured the floors, mopped every surface, and toiled over a bucket full of murky dirt-water. It was still hot out then, and we were caked in grime and sweat within the hour. I had to keep telling myself that this was all for a good purpose: I was going to make room for Him. Living in the West Village, you know that the apartment is the size of a very luxurious shoebox. It was small, yes, but a shoebox that was meant to house some very chic Louboutins. That and, of course, our love. How was I going to squeeze all of our love into this one tiny apartment?

The paintings had to go. They had been terribly important to me at one point or another, and any artist will tell you that their work is like their own flesh and blood. However, I had grown out of whatever place I was in when I painted them back in the day. I was a new man!

I was reborn! Like a phoenix from the ashes (of the cigarette variety, to be precise, in every single corner of the room), I was changing into something more. I was getting rid of all the filth of my former life as a sad and lonely painter. Now I had become the artist who had love and order and cleanliness of body, mind, and soul in his life. I was ready to embark upon my greatest work of art that I had ever hoped to paint: the one of Him and me.

As we sat there on the couch and ate our well-earned Uncle Ted's Modern Chinese food, I was the picture of happiness. I was fresh, and I was new, and I was completely and utterly his. He didn't care that I was caked in dirt, or that I was slurping lo mein feverishly, sending sauce flying. We were just two guys in love, building a home together, and eating Chinese.

To this day, I still keep the little piece of paper from the fortune cookie from that day on a shelf beside my bed. For months afterward, each time I looked at it, I could feel my heart breaking because he wasn't there anymore.

It read: "Cleaning up the past will always clear up the future!"

Then on the back, it taught me how to say the word "Christmas" in Chinese.

Polish National Home
☆ ☆ ☆ ☆ ☆

Categories: Music Venues, Dive Bars, Venues & Event Spaces
Neighborhood: Greenpoint

Our entire courtship was a delicate dance around a minefield of red flags. Although the signs said "stop," I couldn't help but throw myself headlong into the midst of a raucous and volatile affair that would forever change the course of my life. Looking back, I considered what a blatant warning it was that Courtney Love was the person who saved our relationship from burning out too early. Courtney was the reason he fell in love with me, and perhaps one of the reasons why he grew to dislike my *raison d'etre*. It was a hodgepodge of contradiction, but then again, wasn't everything about us? Of course, we had "our song." It was called "Dying," and it was as devastating as it sounded.

Within a month of meeting Him, we had established that we had the potential to become Sid and Nancy. Meeting Him was like a collision of two emotional freight trains running down the same track without brakes or a conductor. It was the summer that I learned to just let go and let my heart speak for itself, even if it was in a reckless and dangerous way. He, of course, was a bit more reserved in his way and kept me at a distance. He'd push me away, we'd fight and yell, then I'd pull away, and he'd grow cold, and I'd tell Him he was wrong, and he'd meet me in the park and we'd just stare at each other from a distance as we inched closer, only to fall into each other's arms and wonder what we were fighting about to begin with. We fought. We fought for a while. But it was never intended to be that way. That's what happens when you put two of the most emotional people in the world, who are extremely similar, in a bag together and drop in the firecracker of one's first summer in New York City. Shit explodes.

I had bought us tickets to see my idol, Courtney Love, perform a show at Warsaw in Greenpoint. It was the venue of my dreams—small, run-down, rustic, oddly Polish, and a little off the beaten path. We had gotten into yet another passionate row the night before the show, and he had sworn me off like he tended to do so easily. The day came, however, and I found myself at Warsaw standing next to Him with a beer in my hand and a crazy smile plastered across my face. No matter the issue at hand, I could just never say no to Him. He was everything I had ever wanted. I looked at Him like I looked at one of my rock idols: I felt in the presence of something that was timeless and legendary that one day I would write songs about.

As the lights lowered at the Warsaw, we pushed our way to the front of the stage. I'd been to many a rock show in my life, but I had never felt such electricity in the air before. I imagined this was what it felt like to be a sixteen-year-old girl at a One Direction show. I couldn't tell if it was Him or me or Courtney that was raising the stakes to a new high. My heart beat like a locomotive, and my temperature rose until my forehead was damp with anxious sweat. I looked over at Him standing next to me and saw that heat had taken Him over as well. His beautiful mane of dark brown hair had fallen from its glorious coif and into a pile of sweaty tendrils. I'd never been so attracted to Him before, and I never expected this side of Him to exist. The cute boy from the park and the coffee shop and the West Village was standing next to me at the rock show to end all rock shows. I grabbed his hand and began to scream wildly as Courtney took to the stage and hoisted her guitar like only Courtney could.

The show was an epic mire of beer and screaming and sweat and moshing. Every so often I would catch myself turning to him like a child at Disneyland would turn to his parent as if to ask "Did you see that?" about some sparkle, or firework, or character. The best part of the entire night was that he saw, for the first time, who I really was. And from the looks of it, he really liked it. His smile spoke volumes—it pushed me to scream even louder, to jump higher, and to push harder into the frenzy that enveloped us.

As time wore on, eventually he would come to criticize me for the person he met there on that night at the Warsaw. He grew harsh and rigid when I raised my middle finger to conformity and a life of structure. My life was a mosh pit, and at times he wished it were an office cubicle. He worried that I would forever be that sweaty hellion that would never clean up enough to make it "in the real world."

The real world was overrated, and I knew it from the start. I wanted to live in that moment at the Warsaw, basking in the greatness of rock and roll royalty forever. There were still aftershocks of that night for months after, and I could close my eyes and remember how I turned to Him as Courtney began to sing "For Once in Your Life." I looked

Him dead in the eye and began to cry tears of joy because I'd never been happier in my life. I'd never come close to something so perfect and so rare as this, and I held it in my hand and kissed it on the mouth.

"Please stick around and I'll build you a world," Courtney sang.

I vowed to do just that.

Minetta Tavern
☆ ☆ ☆ ☆ ☆

Categories: French, American (New), Breakfast & Brunch
Neighborhood: Greenwich Village

The West Village is the most romantic place on earth. This is an undisputed fact for anyone who has been here in the springtime with a person they love. I sometimes have a hard time putting into words exactly why, but I'm pretty sure it has something to do with the way the sunlight filters through the leaves on the tree-lined streets and onto the flesh that has been newly kissed by sunlight after a long winter of melting into the color of buttermilk. It has a lot to do with that feeling of rebirth.

I've lived on what I consider to be the best street in all of Manhattan for almost four years now. Minetta Lane is the most pristine, quiet, quaint, and tree-lined block in all of the West Village. Save for a few occasional drunkards stumbling over from Macdougal Street, it's always completely bare of traffic by both foot and car. It's been the backdrop for many pivotal moments in my young life. In the summer, I walked down it arm and arm with Him, giddy with laughter and excitement til we literally fell into the middle of the street to lie there. We just laid there in the middle of the street and kissed. He lay on top of me and pressed me down hard into the asphalt to the point of it almost hurting and stared into my eyes between passionate kisses and laughter. It must have been a sight to see for the tourist groups that sometimes walk down the street. "And on your left, in typical Greenwich Village fashion, we see two homosexuals in their native habitat performing their elusive courting ritual: the middle-of-the-street make-out."

In the winter, it was the scene of what I assumed would be the last time I ever saw Him. He had fallen to the ground amidst the fallen leaves and curled up into a tiny ball of hysteria. So many times he sobbed how sorry he was and how he didn't want me to leave. I was going to California the next day. My heart had been broken, and my trust betrayed. As beautiful as it was and no matter how much I adored it, Minetta Lane would be the death of me were I to stay. I wouldn't be able to walk down my very own street without thinking of Him and all that he had meant to me. I would always think of the summer, and not the winter that I found out that he was a liar and a cheat and didn't want to commit to being in love with me. I had to get the hell out of there.

On the corner of the street is Minetta Tavern, another backdrop for one of our many passionate rows. I had picked Him up from work; he was starving as usual. It was raining out, and in tow I carried a small jade plant that I had bought Him for his apartment, which was desolate and completely barren of life. Naturally, the jade plant ended up living at my place anyway, as he was never even at his own apartment. We were inseparable. Yet somehow that night, over a deliciously decadent Black Label Burger for which they are so famous, we came to blows over the same issue that we always did: his need to see other people. As always, it crushed me. I couldn't, for the life of me, understand how he couldn't see that the person who went shopping in the rain for a beacon of joy for his life was, in fact, the person that he should be with. Call it addiction to the attention from other men, call it selfishness, call it cold, call it what you will. I just couldn't wrap my head around it. I wanted to be the one so badly.

So we ate our burgers angrily just to get out of there as soon as possible. It was everything they say about the famed Black Label Burger. It was luxurious and rich and satisfying—just like my decadent little street in the West Village. As he fumed at me from across the table and spat out his standard criticism about my puritanical ways for needing a commitment, I sat and thought about what was going on outside. My back began to ache with a phantom pain of being crushed beneath his weight in the middle of the street, and my lips began to chap as his kisses suddenly dried and withered away.

Chapter Three

IT WOULDN'T HAVE HAPPENED with anyone else. All of these rose-colored daydreams and adventures wouldn't have happened with an ordinary man. There was something about Him that drove me wild, and I struggled every day to put my finger on exactly what it was. This freak, this weirdo, this walking funhouse of a man did something to me that made me lose control over my rational mind. Sure, I'd loved before—largely and intensely, with no holds barred. There was something different about loving Him that made all of the insanity seem to make sense.

The whole business of love was a skewed concept to begin with. I had been led to believe that it would happen in a very specific way that had been depicted in fairytales since the dawn of time. I had learned to look for love through my upbringing, which, the more I thought about it, seemed increasingly like a stretch from reality. I thought of my parents, who were still married and wildly in love. They never had to think about each other emailing pictures of their buttholes to ex-lovers at the swipe of a finger just because they felt like it. There was something much simpler about how and why they decided to stay together and form the bond that had kept them as partners for all of these years.

When one thinks of fairytales, one doesn't tend to think of all of the bullshit that came along with forming a relationship in 2013. This modern love—it had to deal with all kinds of deal-breakers: cell phones, social media, apps. These "breakthroughs" in how we related to each other had changed the way we experienced this so-called "real life." We see each other's lives through a carefully curated kaleidoscope of selfies, pictures of coffees, and suggestive poses that best capture every angle needed to stir a desire.

The world was becoming more and more deeply entrenched in the vast nothingness of the Internet. This was of course proven as even I, once a shy and private person by nature, began to splatter my love story on the forum of Yelp. Once I had begun to expose myself, it became like a drug to me. It was an almost instantaneous catharsis, as quick-hitting as heroin and just as numbing. Our private lives, although anonymous and hidden in plain sight, became suddenly "real" as I put them into words. The cups of coffee, the walks in the park, the kissing under flickering streetlamps—all were no longer the precious and private moments that I wanted to remember forever in my mind. Now they were something "concrete" that I could conjure into the forefront of my memory at the click of a button.

Before all of this, there was a time in our history that was simple and quiet. In the first week of our courtship, he lost his iPhone in the back of a cab as we were drunkenly buzzing around the West Village in full swoon. After we returned to my apartment, cloudy with

Negroni-haze and infatuation, he just stared into my eyes as we lay in my bed caressing each other and kissing. He said it didn't matter that he lost his phone. I was the only person he ever called anyway, and I was right there in front of Him, on top of Him, and inside of Him every minute of every day. He had no need to capture every stupid and beautiful moment we shared in a sepia filter to share with the world at large. We existed in real time, rarely apart long enough to consider the notion of missing each other.

He ended up going more than a month without a phone, and it was a dream come true. By instinct, he would know where to find me at any given point in the day, like when I would be done with work and he would be waiting for me patiently outside, smoking cigarettes and fidgeting like a dog waiting for its owner to come out. During this part of our relationship, we did not capture our intense and insane love, and we did not share pictures and status updates on our respective social medias. It was private and real and only our own. It belonged to only me and Him, and this was the happiest I would ever be in the entirety of our relationship.

Time passed, and he eventually got a phone again. Eventually, he used his phone to reconnect with a digital world that was far beyond the boundaries of the little love-bubble we had created together. We both did. He would download Grindr while I was at work and talk to his fans and admirers on Facebook and Instagram, and I would tell the world of Yelp why I had loved Him so madly. He would contact his ex-boyfriends and tell them he missed them, and I would gush about how my heart filled with limitless joy watching Him eat pastrami sandwiches. It was a tough pill to swallow when I eventually learned that it was not the Internet itself that was to blame for the downfall of our love but how we as individuals chose to use it.

Our love story existed in a strange and ultra-modern way. Perhaps it was a sign of the times, and this was how love was to evolve for all of us. I struggled to recall what it was like before all of the mess that technology made of the heart.

On one particular day, he was having one of his regular fits of panic while we were taking a walk through the village. I held his hand as we walked and tried to calm his nerves with my standard brand of idiocy that usually made Him relax or at least smile or laugh. It was spring-time, and the trees in the village were bursting with big bouquets of pink fluff. Releasing his hand, I ran up to one of the pink clouds that was shedding cotton-candy–like confetti on the sidewalk beneath it. Giving little care to the fact that I knew that it would make me filthy and covered in dirt, I lay down on the sidewalk and began to roll around in the petals. His face lit up with that smile that I lived to conjure, and he stood above me. He laughed and took pictures of me surrounded by the pink and posted them on his Instagram with some stupid lit-tle caption about being in love or in spring or something. Of course he would delete it from his feed within days after one of his typical eleventh-hour breakups, and my stain on his cyber life would be only a distant memory. But I still had pink petals showing up in my laundry long after the fact.

Even though I knew I was delete-able from his life, I struggled to find a way to keep what had really happened between us in my life. We got tattoos that would forever mark our bodies with the memory of the beautiful disaster we curated with the brilliant backdrop of New York City. On his forearm he got a tattoo that memorialized the day we spent at the aquarium in Coney Island, eating hot dogs and ice cream and feeling alive. I got mine on my arm, too, to commemorate the special days we spent together in Tompkins Square Park drinking coffee and existing in unison. These were the things that could never be deleted or hidden from our timeline. These were the permanent stories our skin would tell even after we tried to forget that they ever happened. As foolish as it may have been, I wanted it to be known that I wanted it to be forever. I never wanted to forget that before all of the lies and cheating and blame and tears and hunger and hurt, there was something between us that had lit my life on fire.

French Roast

☆ ☆ ☆ ☆ ☆

Category: French

Neighborhood: Greenwich Village

When you're trying to form a life while living in Manhattan, restaurants become the stage on which all sorts of scenes can take place. It becomes so much more than going out to grab a bite to eat to sustain yourself; it becomes so much more than nourishment. Restaurants become memories, and it can be hard to break free from some of the ghosts that linger in your local diner. For me, it was evident that I would never return to French Roast without thinking of that day. French Roast would never again be that place where I ate French onion soup and frisee salads at four in the morning. Now it had become French Roast where I spent Thanksgiving that year he broke my heart.

I hadn't eaten a thing in days. Perhaps it was all of the cigarettes I had been chain-smoking, or perhaps I had just lost the will to go on. I was a wreck. How could I not be? It was Thanksgiving, and he had betrayed me so deeply that it felt like the world was coming to a screeching halt. I had never believed Him before when he said that he wasn't sure if he could only be with me, which of course was what I was pushing for. I had tricked myself into believing he would change for me. Our love was that strong. Or so I was led to believe.

I'm famous for acting irrational when hungry—some may call it my greatest character flaw as I am constantly, ravishingly, devastatingly hungry. I'm not a violent drunk, and I don't fly into fits of rage when I imbibe in anything mood altering. But hunger does something to me that I still can't get a hold of after all my years living on this planet. After not eating for days and wallowing in my own misery on a day that was meant for bountiful, gut-bloating binge eating, I began to feel like I was going to lose my mind. However, nothing even sounded good to me. If I could never eat with Him again at "our place" on St. Mark's, then I would gladly lie down and savor the exquisite pain of my hunger.

Earlier that day, I had called my family in a state of utter panic. Mom picked up the phone, and I began to sob and wail hysterically in the kind of cacophony that is usually reserved for infants or the mortally wounded. Through gurgling agony, I choked out the words "This day is my favorite. I just want some turkey." Translation: I can't believe he ruined everything. If he really loved me, then why would he do such a thing to me?

French Roast was the first place I ever had a drink in New York City. It was the year 2000, and it seemed almost a lifetime ago. The irony was not lost on me, seeing as how it looked to be the last place I might have a drink in New York City as well. It certainly wasn't planned that way. It just sort of happened. After writhing in pain on the couch all day crying, I finally gave in to Him as he had asked to see me before

I left. Being the sucker that I am for punishment, I agreed to take a walk with Him.

It was freezing cold and late at night, and several places had already closed. French Roast is but a stone's throw away from my apartment, so when we passed by it all aglow with flickering candlelight and abuzz with life, it seemed like a no-brainer. We had been there together a few times for late-night dinners and the occasional glass of wine at the bar. Instantly, I began to get vivid and debilitating flashbacks of happier times. I remembered how we sat side by side in the booth on one of our first dates and how hard I became as my hand grabbed his knee under the table. It's so easy to remember all the good sometimes. It's a blessing and a curse.

Thanksgiving 2013 will always be remembered. Every little detail will forever be burned into my brain like a tattoo. I can remember the taste of the pumpkin ravioli that I ordered because it seemed like the most seasonally festive thing to have. I'm sure it was delicious, but it tasted like sawdust to me. He ordered the boeuf bourguignon and couldn't get more than two bites down at a time without breaking into tears. It especially upset Him when I handed Him the basket of sliced baguette to sop up all of the delicious sauce that was left in the bottom of the bowl. He knew that I knew exactly what he liked. It was devastating. It was the worst night of my life. It was probably the worst because we both knew that after that meal we would never be allowed to return to being ourselves again.

None of this is French Roast's fault. It was all just us being us. Me, drinking corked burgundy, and Him, having a total emotional meltdown that was making the two girls dining next to us totally uncomfortable. I can only pity the poor, sweet waiter who had to pretend to not notice the two guys crying and holding each other at table 15. The air was so thick with tension that it seemed to disturb the mood of the entire room.

That being said, French Roast will forever hold a place in my heart. It was the first and the last, the alpha and the omega, of my once whimsical heart.

Then I went to California.

Nathan's Famous

☆ ☆ ☆ ☆ ☆

Categories: American (Traditional), Hot Dogs
Neighborhood: Coney Island

"Stop!" I screamed at the top of my lungs.

The cab came to a screeching halt in the middle of 6th Avenue. It was early in the morning, so this was okay. We hadn't made it more than a few blocks from my apartment, but I already needed to go back. I made the driver circle around and instructed him to leave the meter running as I dashed hastily into my building, nearly slipping and toppling over on the ice that dressed the curb. I ran up the five flights to my apartment. Out of breath and light headed, I threw open my door and ran to the shelf.

I stopped to marvel for a moment at the little shelf that was right above my bed. There, sitting front and center, was the thing that I had forgotten. My lucky charm. My prized possession. The one thing that was going to guarantee that the plane I was about to board would not fall out of the sky in mid-flight and end my sordid affair on this planet. How could I have forgotten it, especially on this important day when I was traveling across the entire country? I had remembered to put it in my pocket every day when I got dressed, so what was so different about today?

I snatched it out of its shrine on the shelf and secured it in my fifth jean pocket, where it lived most of the time. At least when I was wearing pants.

My lucky penny was my newest obsession. It's a stupid little thing—one of those things you get when you go to an amusement park or a fair and you place a penny in the machine and turn the crank. It flattens the penny and stretches it out and embosses a little picture on it. Mine? It's a jellyfish. It's from the Coney Island Aquarium. And it reminds me of the best summer of my entire life.

See, I'm no hoarder, and that's what's weird about this whole ordeal. Most of my prized possessions are simple memories, and these are the things that will never weigh me down or make me feel trapped should I ever get the sudden urge to move to Europe. Or California. Or become a missionary or a monk who lives in a monastery somewhere on a big, snowy mountaintop in Tibet. That's why it's so strange that I've started to keep things that he gave to me.

On the shelf in the shrine is where the penny lives when I'm not wearing pants. Next to that are a few flimsy pieces of paper from fortune cookies that we ate together. Nearby are a few black-and-white photo strips from happier times and the stupid plush dog he won for me on that trip to Coney Island where the penny was born. Like any scar or tattoo or chemical burn, these trinkets were now a permanent fixture on the topography of my life. He had always had such a thing for "things," and perhaps I did now, too.

These days, I didn't feel much like myself. I knew that the summer, and our relationship, had ended in an utter disaster of epic proportions, but I was determined not to let it get the best of me. That's why I kept these things, and instead of setting them on fire or mailing them back to Him like I probably should have, I decided to make them into something far less sinister.

These were my new motivation, my new reason to carry on. These things were a reminder that I wasn't dead inside and that I had lived and loved and felt like the person that I had always wanted to be. Even though it was long gone, I would never let myself forget how alive and happy and loved I felt that summer. Sure, he was a scumbag that lied to me constantly and cheated on me and used me and emotionally abused me—but that's where the real glory lies. Those would not be the things that defined our love, as dead and distant as it was. I chose a new memory and let all of those bad ones just melt away. I had thought I found The One, and this propelled me to become the best version of myself that I had ever met.

We had destroyed each other fully. No one can contest that. But none of that would ever erase that day on Coney Island. It won't erase my penny or my stuffed dog or that feeling I get when I think about eating at Nathan's Hot Dogs with Him. There was hardly anyone on the boardwalk, and it felt like we were the only two people that even mattered in all of New York. It's that kind of stuff that I'll take with me as I go—not all of that nasty stuff that mired us down and made us into ugly, hateful people.

I decided to take the penny with me wherever I went for the rest of my life. I would keep it in my pocket as a reminder that I had the ability to love unconditionally. It wasn't a reminder of love lost, but rather a reminder that love existed. Someday, someone would take me and my weird little rituals seriously. I knew that the summer of 2013 wasn't the last time I would go to Nathan's and be wildly and hopelessly in love. I'd go back there. In a heartbeat. Even if only to savor the best damn hot dog in all of New York. Even by myself.

As the plane took off, I held the penny in my hand and squeezed it. I could feel my heart lighten, or perhaps it was just the altitude rushing blood to my brain. It was time to let go.

Sunset Tower Hotel

☆ ☆ ☆ ☆ ☆

Category: Hotels
Neighborhood: West Hollywood

The bathtub in the Sunset Tower Hotel was roughly the size of my apartment back home in the arctic tundra of Manhattan. As I lay back into the scalding hot water, I could feel the weight of the world slowly melt away from my skin. Across the bathroom was a floor-to-ceiling window that overlooked the boxy totality of Beverly Hills, and it just sat there. For a moment, I was silent, and the big marble room seemed to fill with the deafening cacophony of nothing. I mused on the iconic words of Brett Easton Ellis from his opus *Less Than Zero*: disappear here.

Perhaps someday I could. For the time being, I was more than content with my sick love affair with New York. She was the bane of my existence in the wintertime, but I knew that soon I would be taking long walks through the tree-lined streets of the West Village with a smile on my face, an iced coffee in my hand, and the soundtrack to Amelie blaring through my headphones reminding me of my truest self. Now, in Los Angeles, I almost felt the same sense of ease. Being here brought me a kind of whimsy that seemed almost like it was borrowed. As I sat in the huge tub, I skimmed a handful of bubbles from the surface and fashioned myself a bubble-beard and a Kiehl's shampoo mohawk. I looked at myself for a solid five minutes in the mirror above the tub and wondered who I was and who I was going to become because of this trip.

Los Angeles is not a place to go and "find yourself." I'd known this for most of my young life, as I was raised not far from these very palm trees lining the boulevard beneath my hotel window. After living in New York City for so long, LA was a place where I went when I needed to lose myself. It was a place where I could go and shed my dour demeanor that I wore like a bawdy velveteen sports coat. It was so loud, and so blatantly worn on me, that it felt heavy and emotionally cumbersome. When I needed to remind myself not to take myself too seriously, I would always have this strange little oasis of sheer vapidity and vanity to put things into perspective.

I woke up early on the second day of my trip and watched the sun rise. The balcony of the room was one of the most stunning views I'd ever taken in. To the east I could see (and nearly hear) the hustle and bustle of Santa Monica Boulevard—the epicenter of gay West Hollywood. To the west lay downtown LA, a big cluster of sharp looking skyscrapers huddled together on the vast flat canvas of city. Further west I could make out the Griffith Park Observatory up on the hill, and I began to reminisce of happier times when I was there with boys who thought they loved me at one point or another. This place was not my home, but the histories that I had written here spoke volumes and felt oddly familiar and comforting.

As I said, it was not my intention to find myself here. I already felt as if I had a very firm grasp on who I was and what I wanted. I was here because I wanted to reaffirm that I was doing the right thing. At thirty-one years of age, I felt lost in the tangled mess of Manhattan and what had become of my personal life. Manhattan was so blatantly cumbersome that it was taking over my entire body's equilibrium. It was just too much sadness and hurt and happy memories turned sour by deceit. While I was here, basking in the bastard sun and taking in unseasonal rosé, I could shed that skin and just be.

I knew I had to return shortly, but I just reminded myself to breathe and remember who I was. I had lost myself somewhere deep in a snow-drift, but being thawed out was helping me remember all that had been before. I would return to Manhattan not a new person, but the person I had always been before all of the pain and all of the sadness. I'd still crave Him and want Him endlessly, but I'd crave myself and my once-ardent life more. When I returned, I'd plant palm trees in my heart. I'd wear emotional flip-flops and bleach the tips of my soul. I'd think of the morning view from Sunset Tower and pray that I could be a better person. Change is good. Change is vital. But I would never, for any man, city, or situation, change the truest desire in my heart to celebrate and revel in the power of true love—for myself and for others.

Chapter Four

IT WAS WITH FREAKISH BRAVADO that I carried around my heartbreak. As they say about wearing one's heart on one's sleeve, it means to be wide open and honest with one's feelings. It made me wonder if wearing a *broken* heart on one's sleeve was even a thing. Why did I do it? Why couldn't I put on a fake smile and drink my way through the recovery period like a normal person going through a breakup? Why was it that instead of holding my head high and realizing my self-worth, I just wore that sour feeling of misery like a scarlet letter?

I did my best to hide it when I was forced to leave the solitude of my warm little cave of an apartment. I kept melodramatic Facebook posts to a minimum, and when asked by friends how I was doing, I was able to feign a quiet "fine" and change the topic. As much as I tried to play it off that I wasn't slowly rotting inside, I still had to deal with it in my own way. Between bouts of writhing around in tear-soaked fits of release that escaped every now and then, I would sit at my laptop and wait for the strength to churn out some of the caged emotions onto Yelp. Like a flasher in the streets, I got a momentary kick of validation as I streaked my way through the random corridors of the Internet with my emotional dick hanging from beneath my metaphorical trench coat.

Then I'd have irrational freak-outs that would sideswipe me out of nowhere. Maybe I deserved it. Maybe he was right in saying that if I would have just given Him some space, and maybe took a little better care of myself and gone to the gym a little more, he wouldn't have even wanted to cheat on me. It was something he swore upon every time we fought—it was clearly my fault that he cheated on me. Because I wasn't being what he wanted, he wasn't being what he wanted as a result. That and, of course, the fact that I was too much "fun."

He hated how much fun we had together, and I figured this must be a result of some kind of fucked-up upbringing of his. Perhaps it said a lot about my character that I do, in fact, love to take life far less seriously than it should be taken—at least when I'm in a good mood. My ideal life goals include finding a way to stay in bed all day watching funny movies with a man, only taking breaks to run to the freezer for more ice cream or to take a sexual intermission. Given my way, I would spend every afternoon walking through the park sipping coffee, reading the newspaper, and picking my nose with wild abandon.

I believed in working to live, not living to work. He was always so pissed off when I was just sitting there wearing only pajamas and a shit-eating grin with my pint of ice cream in hand—he had to be out fixing his life, chasing his dreams, and making himself a different kind of person. He had to be out there making a name for himself and getting "liked." He hated me because my life was secretly how he wished he could live his life, but he had been hardwired from youth to work hard and change or he'd never "make it" in the end. Me? I thought I'd already made it. I thought I had it all—love and happiness and fun and all of the time in the world to just sit and exist without wanting anything more from the beast that Manhattan could be.

I never asked for much: just a best friend, some good snacks, a few laughs, and dick on the regular. It's the New American Dream.

Although I was only four years older than Him, at times I felt like I was completely out of touch with his entire way of looking at the world. The small gap of age was the difference between someone who existed in the age of the Internet versus someone who remembered living life before the age of the Internet.

He was always so obsessed with getting "likes" on everything. If it were a picture of Him (usually topless and flexing his bulging biceps or chest) he would check his phone manically as to make sure all of his followers were impressed. I'd sit by his side all the while and try to pet his arms IRL, and he'd swat me away.

"I like you! I like you IRL! I like you so much, and I can touch you physically and kiss you *right now!*" I'd scream silently from the sidelines as I grabbed at Him and tried to squeeze affection from Him. Exhausted from his dead stare into the pixelated world of his Internet empire, I'd finally give in and pick up my own phone. I'd click the little thumbs-up icon, and then he'd look up and smile at me.

How the fuck did we get here?

There were times when I was convinced that he and I were the exact same person. We loved the same things, had the same sense of humor and general understanding, and saw the world in our own special way. Then again, there were times when I believed that he must certainly be an alien from another planet. Or was it I who was the weirdo? I couldn't ever speak to Him on the matter, so I must assume that it was me.

A few months after he and I broke up, I began therapy.

As I made my way uptown to the Institute for Contemporary Psychotherapy, I couldn't help but scoff at the acronym: ICP. Coincidentally (or perhaps not) it was the same as the horrifying band of nightmarish clowns known as Insane Clown Posse. You'd know them if you saw a picture of them—they're the freak shows with the terrifying fans that dress up in spikey metal garb and paint their faces in dripping black-and-white clown makeup.

"Fantastic," I said to myself as I ascended from the subway in Colombus Circle. "I'm an emotional Juggalo."

I was fully prepared to do what I needed to do to begin to sort out all of the madness that had occurred as a result of losing my mind in a stupid love affair. I took full ownership of the fact that it had indeed come to the point where I could no longer go about my life without trying to crack the code as to what had brought me to this place of complete and utter despair. The proud son of a bitch that I was, I had never really thought that it would come to needing a shrink, but alas, there I was. Before I knew it, I was sitting on the couch of the good Dr. Bob. His two scraggly Jack Russell terriers ran circles around me and used me as a jungle gym, leaving their wiry white hairs all over my carefully curated all-black ensemble that seemed ever so fitting for the occasion.

Dr. Bob seemed like a nice enough guy, I figured. He had a very knowing look about himself—the cardigans he wore, the thin wire glasses, and the graying beard. He looked, in every sense, like the type of man I assumed a therapist would look like. He was kind and contemplative and utterly polite—in fact, almost too so. Part of me was waiting for Dr. Bob to get in there with the really hard-hitting questions that would strike me like a ton of bricks and force me into one of those "breakthroughs" where I would collapse into a puddle and be all like "Of course! Why didn't I see it all along? I love me! *I love me!*"

Bob was great, and I saw him for a few months. Although it was like second nature for me to tell Bob all the sordid details of my relationship with Him, which was the cause of my having to seek out therapy to go on with my life, that was not the heart of the matter that Bob was trying to crack open. Dr. Bob wanted to know about my childhood and my family and what it was like for me running away from home as a teenager to make it in the big city.

I wracked by brain trying to answer the doctor truthfully. For whatever reason, I had a hard time remembering the details of how exactly I had come to be in the place I currently resided in. Truthfully, I couldn't remember the how or the why that had set me up to be the catatonic mess that sat before him decked out in full mourning attire for the death of my wayward heart.

So much drama.

Dr. Bob wanted to know everything about my family life and what it was like growing up in Southern California. Moreover, he wanted to know why I had come to New York City in the first place. As far as I could remember, the answer was simple: I came to New York City to be in love.

It was the truth, as corny as it sounded. Near the end of high school, I began dating a very severe boy, a few years older than I, who made me want to do crazy things. I was not yet eighteen years old, and as my family was still learning how to deal with the whole "gay thing," most of our relationship was kept shrouded in secrecy. I snuck out of the house in the night to drive around with him and kiss in his car, and I wrote him long letters that described in gory detail the darkest of my teenage carnal longing for him. We slept together at friends' places who would have us—the whole thing was very Capulet and Montague. All the while, I yearned for an independence that would allow me to live out (what felt like it at the time) that burning teenage romance.

He was a tall and angular boy, dark and shadowed in mystery and sharp edges. He read and lived his life by the words of a man called Oscar Wilde, and I was enamored with the unconventional philosophies he rattled off. His wild heart and his thin and scruffy face and the long cigarettes he smoked enraptured me in a way little old me had never known before. I wasn't sure if he was my first love or perhaps my first obsession or something that I had not yet developed language to describe. Regardless, all I knew was that I would follow him wherever he went—for I knew that wherever he was would be a place where I could be free from the conventional shackles of my sheltered life at home.

It seemed so casual at the time.

He said, "We should move to New York."

I said, "Sure."

The next thing I knew I was sleeping on a couch in a tiny little living room with him wrapped in my arms, and the brilliant and foreign light of Brooklyn was shining down upon us. The apartment belonged to some friends of his—an exotic poet girl who had ferocious opinions and feelings that scared the shit out of me and enthralled me at the same time, and her boyfriend who was in the musical "Stomp!" over on St. Mark's Place. I envied them both. They drank a lot and seemed to really love each other, and even when they fought (which they did fairly often) I felt like they were the most adult and responsible peers I had ever come across. Crashing on their couch, I felt like I, too, was finally a real-life adult.

It was no more than a month before I broke up with the man I traveled across the country with. He had a hard time finding work in the city and an equally hard time finding himself. Perhaps the reality of the situation became too much for him—but I had gone into full-blown survival mode. I was desperate to not give up or give in. With the dregs of money we had left, we bought pasta at the grocery store to live off of. I walked slowly behind him and stole packets of dehydrated sauce that required only water to make. Although looking back it seemed like a desperate time, I knew it was just me doing what I had to do to build my foundation.

Shortly after my boyfriend left, the Twin Towers fell. He was back in California, and I hunkered down and refused to let the world get to me. Alone and confused in Manhattan, I climbed to the roof of our shitty little sublet in Washington Heights and watched as the world changed forever. The reasonable thing to do would have been to pack what few belongings I had and crawl back West. It was what everyone had expected, in fact.

Instead, I stayed. Determined to carve out a new life for myself, I toiled my way through a series of odd jobs to get by. I made coffee, I waited tables, I bartended, and I had a weird, brief foray into the world of go-go dancing and DJing. The tales of that period in my life were enough material to pique Dr. Bob's curiosity as to what had set me so strangely in my way, but that wasn't the heart of the matter that had turned me into the man I had become. Bob was very inquisitive as to my early life before New York that built me into the creature I was. He wanted to know about my family and my early hopes and dreams and why it was that I felt the need to find a man to complete what I had considered a life half-full.

When I shaved my hair into a gigantic blond mohawk and hauled my skinny ass up to the tops of bars and dancing platforms, I was blatantly rebelling against the world I had come from. In my young mind, I sought to curate a life that was seemingly rejected by the wholesome life I had left in California. My parents were one of the few couples I had ever known that were not torn asunder by the ravages of divorce, and I thought about this a lot. They were (and had always been) truly and madly in love. Dad would look at my mom with stars in his eyes and felt no hesitation to share with my younger brother and me how deeply in love he was with her. It was like they were two separate parts of a great big whole that didn't make sense when apart. They completed each other, and raised a beautiful—albeit modest—home rich with love and value.

It was not shocking to find that I desperately craved that kind of companionship. I wanted, with all of my heart, to build a home and a family the way that my parents had. I believed in true love and soulmates because it was the only kind of family I had ever known. The stakes in our respectable causes, however, were blatantly varied to a staggering extreme. I vied for the capability to emulate that beautiful portrait of family but in my own way and on my own terms.

It wasn't rocket science. None of it was. I began to wonder what the hell I was doing every week as I made my way uptown to see Dr. Bob. I knew why I was the way I was, and I knew exactly where I was coming from. The only thing I didn't understand was why I felt so broken and depressed in the wake of Him leaving me. I'd not wanted the doctor's advice as to how to rebuild myself—I wanted a fix. I wanted to hear from Bob that it was a sick and cruel hand of outside force that had wrecked me. I wanted confirmation that I'd not been a fool for giving away my heart, but rather a fool for giving it to the wrong person.

Basically, I wanted Dr. Bob to grab me by the shoulders, shake me violently, and say, "Fuck that asshole! It wasn't your fault that he was a lying, cheating, abusive scumbag! You are better than this!"

Instead, I chose to turn to drugs.

It was easier, and I thought it would just make more sense. I spoke to my doctor of my paralyzing bouts of anxiety that I felt every time I thought of Him. I told him how I couldn't get out of bed most mornings and how I had grown weak and thin due to my inability to eat. He just jotted down notes on his yellow legal pad like he'd heard my story countless times. I'd never taken medication before, and I was excited at the prospect of the magical little pills repairing the cracks in my fucked-up little situation. Ideally, I felt like I needed a full skin transplant—but perhaps a few mood stabilizers would do for now.

It was nothing new to me feeling gloomy in the wintertime, but this was different. It was desperate. There was nothing I wouldn't do to be rid of the nagging hurt that clung to me like a straightjacket. So I took the prescribed pills and I waited.

The thing about antidepressants is that they *work*. After a few weeks of taking the tiny little pills, I no longer felt like I had the world collapsing around me. The problem that I came to encounter, however, was that I felt nothing at all. Suddenly, I could get out of bed, and eventually I began to eat again, but I felt like a spectator viewing myself in recovery from my position floating on the ceiling above myself. After weeks of this newfound numbness, I returned to my doctor and tried to tell him that I missed feeling things—the good things at least. His answer, of course, was to take some more pills in addition to the ones I was already taking. He said they'd just take the "zombie state" away and make me feel a little more lively. I opened the hatch and swallowed those, too, and waited for feelings to come back.

I waited for something to change, but even through the therapy and the pills, I was still held hostage by the city that loomed around me. I wondered what else I could do to stifle the process that was driving me crazy. Sadly, I could come up with no answers. I kept on my way and dragged myself through the big graveyard city and hoped that something, anything, would feel like home again.

Veselka

☆ ☆ ☆ ☆ ☆

Categories: Diners, Ukrainian
Neighborhood: East Village

Comfort food has always been a New York thing.

Being that this city has been filled with people coming from all over the world to make their dreams come true, it's hard to come by a native New Yorker these days. Especially in the winter, it can seem like one big lonely mass of orphans. Like moths to a flame, all of the orphans search long and far for something that makes them feel at home. Nine out of ten times, all it takes is a warm cup of soup and a sandwich to make you remember being at mom's house.

Veselka has been a shining beacon of comfort amidst the cold embrace of Manhattan for the past sixty years. For me, it's always been the embodiment of a really comfortable pair of jeans. Its casual ambience and unintentional ease has always felt like a warm hug to me. Like coming home, I think of cups of black coffee and piping hot pierogies and get all fuzzy feeling. There's just something about it that I can't put my finger on. Much like anything else in this city, it's probably just all of the memories that fill the room.

We spend most of our lives here in Manhattan longing to find comfort. If we don't find something that rings familiar, then we might as well be lost—just a long line of sickened immigrants trying to make it happen in a cold and foreign land. I've had several spots like this scattered all around downtown New York for the past thirteen years. I've found those spots that feel like home and made them my own, and I guess that's what it means to make a life for oneself. I never expected it, but when I return to California for the holidays, I find myself yearning to be sitting at a booth in Veselka. Screw Mom's homemade tamales. Now comfort food to me is a cup of matzo ball soup made by a large Ukrainian woman (probably) named Oksana.

Comfort is such a double-sided sword, though, isn't it? Just when you get comfortable enough to really give yourself to another person, you begin to look slovenly, like you've given up. That was never the way with Him and I—I always pulled myself together for Him. Every time I went to pick Him up from work, I looked like I was ready to walk the runway, because I cared. We were comfortable, yes, but I never cracked a fart in front of Him the whole time we dated. I wanted to be sexy for Him in a way that I had never wanted before, and it terrified me. Perhaps true comfort is letting the other person see every single side of you, even if it's not flattering. Even if it's lukewarm soup, it still feels like home.

I awoke in a panic in Gramercy with a Shiba Inu staring down my nose and looking quizzically at me as if I had been snoring or something. I'd not seen Lola since she was a puppy, and that was nearly ten years ago. With a panic in my head I shot up out of bed and ran to collect my clothing. My phone had died, and splayed out on the bed like a ragdoll was a man who I had dated when I first moved to New York.

No matter how distant I felt from him, it was oddly familiar to be back in his presence again after such a long hiatus. It was what I had sought out the minute I knew that The One would never want me the way I had wanted Him. It was comfort food. I ran wounded and flailing into the arms of someone who knew me for who I was, or at least used to be. No matter how wrong it felt, I did it because all I knew was that I wanted to be desired. All the while, it was Him in my head. Him in between every sentence uttered to my ex. Him begging and pleading for me to get him a cup of coffee. Him looking at me like his best friend. And most importantly, Him in the first real snow of the season that was coming down in buckets outside the picturesque window over 24th Street. It put a dent in my heart like I had never felt before in my entire life. I knew I had to escape immediately before I made a fool of myself.

Being comfortable suddenly had never felt more uncomfortable in my entire life. A pang of hunger resonated in my stomach, and I immediately felt an uncontrollable craving for pierogies.

As much as I hated it, I knew I had to make my way through the snow to the New York Public Library. A promise was a promise.

New York Public Library, Stephen A. Schwarzman Building
☆ ☆ ☆ ☆ ☆

Category: Libraries
Neighborhood: Midtown East

I've never set foot inside of the New York Public Library in Midtown. I've always wondered if it is as grandiose on the inside as it is on the outside. All I've ever known about the inside of this building is that it was where Carrie Bradshaw was supposed to get married in the *Sex and the City* movie, and in typical New York bachelor fashion, her scumbag fiancé leaves her at the altar. In a building that is so full of history, it's quite funny that this is my only point of reference. By funny, I mean sad. And by sad, I mean relatable.

Back when the nights were still somewhat warm from the dying ebb of summer, I came to sit under one of the great lion statues that sat guarding the library. It was the first night that I had spent with Him since he had decided that he didn't want to see me anymore. Masochistic me, I had come running back into his company the moment he came to call. Although I knew he no longer wanted me, I had craved his company endlessly. After a month of not sleeping or eating and writing dozens of unsent letters to Him, it seemed like I was finally getting the chance for some closure. Or he was coming back. Who knew?

He sat me down on a bench beneath the southernmost lion and told me he had something for me. I sat hesitantly and waited for whatever crazy gesture he was going to sling my way. I wasn't sure if it was going to be a wedding ring or fifteen stabs to the chest—typical Him-style. He had always been good about surprises. It blew me away when he handed me his iPhone and played a video he had made for me. With ear buds in, I watched in complete shock as a video played of Him walking through all the places we had been together in the course of our brief affair. From the bar Von where we had our first date to the Temperance Fountain in Tompkins Square Park, which he knew was my favorite place in the entire city. He had spent an entire day on foot revisiting our love and set the whole thing to music. I began to shake uncontrollably, and it was only a matter of seconds before I became hysterical.

I held Him, and he clung to me and kissed my tear-stained face. He told me that he loved me and that he was sorry. In my fragile state, I actually believed Him when he said it was all going to be all right.

The funny thing is, it actually *was* all right after that. We both said we were sorry and continued our beautiful love like it had been actually fortified by our time apart. He said he would appreciate every second I was back in his life like it was a gift, and I said I would always love and want Him. After the tears subsided, we went back to being the most in-love couple New York City had ever seen. I was sideswiped by how thankful I was that he had returned, and it seemed like it had finally sunk in that we were destined to be together.

A few weeks later, we spent the day in Coney Island being wildly in love. We took in the aquarium and the boardwalk and ate ice cream cones, as one does when in Coney Island. My man was back, and I had never known such peace and happiness. Later that night as we walked home from the ferry, we made a promise to each other. We said that the first time it snowed, no matter what we were doing or where we were in life, we would return to the library and meet. It was a promise, and I kissed Him and looked into his eyes to seal the deal.

Two gigantic statues of crouching lions adorn the front steps of the library. These iconic lions of the New York Public Library are named Fortitude (on the north side) and Patience (on the south—our side). I reflected deeply on what this could possibly mean. Even after he had left me for the last time, I knew that I would return to Patience on the first snow. I also knew that he would not be there. But, a promise was a promise, and I knew I had to go—if only to prove to myself that I could. As the snow came down in sheets, I made my way from Times Square and sat beneath the big marble guardian.

I sat on the bench in the snow and froze my ass off. I thought about Patience and what it meant. Did it mean to be patient for Him and to let Him run his course until he was ready to finally be in love? Or did it mean to be patient with myself, and let time heal the wounds that he had knowingly inflicted upon my heart? Either way, time crawled by, and I found myself feeling terribly impatient. I looked up at the lion, which was wearing a Christmas wreath around his thick neck, and wondered how long I had to be patient until all of the pain would go away. Even though he had broken me completely, I had secretly wished that he would be there, standing in the snow with that typical look on his face and his adorable pea coat.

On the north side of the library sat the lion named Fortitude, which I went and sat under as well. Fortitude was the one I should have been sitting under all along. Strength, courage, and grace were the things that were going to save me. I knew that I had done everything I could to save my once ardent heart from being completely snubbed out.

Melvin's Juice Box

☆ ☆ ☆ ☆ ☆

Category: Juice Bars & Smoothies
Neighborhood: Greenwich Village

There is absolutely nothing funny about crushing depression, until the moment comes when absolutely everything is funny about crushing depression.

In a desperate attempt to pull myself out from the bell jar, I went to try and reclaim the happy person I had been in the not-so-distant past. Happiness, I figured, was a palpable object that I had simply left behind like a pair of gloves or a scarf, and it would be waiting there at Melvin's right where I had left it, or perhaps in the lost and found. I went to Melvin's to try and find that happy person I was in the summer—the sun-kissed skin I wore like a trophy and the delicious green juice that I used to drink with Him that tasted like a love potion. I always found Melvin's to be my happy place; what with the constant stream of reggae and vibrant colors everywhere you looked, it was hard to be sad when immersed in such brilliance.

Melvin's was like Xanax for the soul. It calmed me, and made me happy, and I felt that the people who went there or even worked there were "my kind of people." Melvin was usually there during the morning hours, and every time I walked in, he would greet me with a smile and a fist-bump and ask how I was doing. It was a rarity in this neighborhood and in this age to find such natural and honest hospitality. So I went there and hoped to be reunited with my heart, which used to be at peace in this very room where I was now looking for something I had lost.

I could feel the snow drifts outside as if they were glaring at me through the windows. It was as if they could just knock on the door to say, "Don't be fooled by the reggae and the fruit and the colors—we're still here." Inside, Melvin's was warm and welcoming as usual, but as I should've expected, my joy was nowhere to be found. I looked under the tables for it, hoping that it would be in an unmarked package—"If you see something, say something." It just wasn't there. Maybe, like an unattended child, it had been scooped up by a concerned patron who was quick to call 311 and report this tragedy. Who would leave their heart so callously unattended?

The minute the green elixir "The Body Good" touched my lips, I could feel it all coming back to me. It's always been said that the sense of smell holds the strongest connection to memories, but I knew this was not true for me. This fat ass has always been brought home by taste. Just by tasting the bright zing of ginger with the deep earthiness of kale, I could remember every single day of the summer like it was playing before me in IMAX. When I closed my eyes, the snow drifts ceased their knocking at the door, and suddenly I felt like I was wearing one of those white tank tops that I had worn day in and day out. I could remember what it was like waking up in the morning and walking out into the blaring heat completely unfazed, because I knew that the world was my oyster and I had no need of hiding indoors from the winter's cruel hands. That, and of course, Him.

When I was a little boy, my grandma Edna used to sing to me. It was one of the few memories I still had of her. That, and the color of the robes that she used to wear. She was always wearing a very distinct shade of baby blue, almost the kind of blue you see depicted in pictures of the Virgin Mary. She would hug me close and sing to me her favorite song, "You Are My Sunshine."

You are my sunshine, my only sunshine

You make me happy when skies are gray

You'll never know, dear, how much I love you

Please don't take my sunshine away.

I've lived in New York for nearly fourteen years now, and this happens every single year. It's the winter. It destroys me, and I don't know how to fight it. Doubled with heartbreak, this winter seemed that it would be one that I could never bounce back from. He had left with my heart, winter had left with my mind, and my body was left numb and pointless like one of those gross crab carcasses you see washed up on the beach in the summer. I had tried with all of my might to regain the whimsy that the summer had left in my dormant heart, but it was slipping through my fingers like so many grains of sand. All I could taste was the good times and the happiness and the light. But something still pulled at me like a nagging cough that just wouldn't go away.

I looked down at my wrist at the tattoo that I got hundreds of years ago. It read "Edna" in a cursive script. Ink is important to me for a few reasons, but more than decoration (and just because I think it's sexy), it's a reminder. I remembered my grandma, who had passed away many years ago but still lived inside of me. Her legacy and her song would forever be with me and inside of me. My sunshine had been taken away, but it would always be there, lingering deep down inside. Perhaps it was just dormant, and hibernating, as all things tend to do in the winter.

I slugged back my juice and walked out into the cold, praying that summer, and my heart, would return.

Eva's

☆ ☆ ☆ ☆ ☆

Category: Mediterranean
Neighborhood: Greenwich Village

It was time for damage control.

The winter had completely ravaged my body and spirit, and I was poised to sit and wither away in a mire of cheap take-out and Netflix binges. It was the perfect storm of a heartbreak that took me and threatened to pull me asunder. I'd been here in this familiar place before, and I knew by heart the steps to recovery. However, this time I knew that I needed to go about things differently if I didn't want to wind up in the same shipwreck of a life I had come from.

I knew it was time to fix myself. Perhaps it hadn't been Him all along that was sabotaging my hopes and dreams—it frightened me to think that there was a distinct possibility that it had been me and all of my shortcomings. I am, by nature, not a very "hot" guy. Being a gay man in New York City, "hot" is the most important commodity that exists. Maybe my lack of "hotness" was what was constantly putting me at a disadvantage with dating. I'm skinny, I have toothpick arms, and it's a constant battle with the mirror. Through gay evolution, I've formed a defense mechanism against my tragic biology, which has helped me to think that there is a slight possibility that I will not die alone. If I couldn't be one of the muscled, vapid, sex-and-gym-obsessed himbo's that he constantly berated me for not being, then I would just have to settle for my brain. And sometimes my heart. Those were my strong points, and even though he constantly made me feel that that wasn't enough, I knew that there had to be someone out there who thought that it was.

The real kicker was that I (as in my rational and personal self, not my feeble chicken-body) was already good. I knew my heart and my mind backwards and forwards, and I knew what I stood for and what I could not stand. Maybe it really *was* my disgusting girly-boy body that was ruining my life. It just had to be—everything else was in its place. Virtue? Check. Honesty? Check. Loyalty? Check. Kindness? Check. Tenderness? Check. Pectorals . . . pectorals? And the silence is deafening.

This world is a sick and shallow place, and if I wanted to survive, I knew that I had to either sink or swim. I chose to swim. First step was to dip my pinky toe in the shallow end (pun intended) and start to treat my body like I treated my heart—with extra care and tenderness. I went to Eva's Health Food Store and felt like Columbus discovering uncharted territory for the very first time. All around me swarmed muscular gym rats shoveling protein-laden trays of heaping food into their faces. Little old me, I felt like I didn't belong. As per usual.

I couldn't be daunted by this, though. I had to change or I would forever be stuck as just another useless waif in a sea of torsos and rock-hard asses. Anyone could love me for being a good person, and that was all fine and dandy. But at the end of the day, I knew the only real way to find and keep a man was to fix myself up to not *look* like I had a heart or a brain. I'd wallowed in my condition long enough to know that kale, brown rice, vegetables, and a shit-ton of protein was going to save my life.

When I went to Eva's and spoke to the guy at the counter about getting some protein powder to help me gain weight, I felt like he thought he was being punked. Every journey starts with a single step, so I bought a gigantic barrel of protein and lugged it to the counter. The tub of powder itself was nearly as large around as I was, and I felt like a cartoon as I schlubbed it with me. I had to keep telling myself over and over again that this was all going to be worth it someday. Someday, I would be looked at as more than just another nice guy. Someday, all this quinoa and chicken breast would erase the memory of how good the cheeseburger at the Spotted Pig tastes. I took home an order of grilled chicken with steamed vegetables and brown rice and pretended that I was eating a pulled-pork sandwich.

I wished that someone could love me for who I was, but immediately thought better of myself and realized that it's a crock of shit. No one would ever love me if I stayed the same because I could never love myself. All I ever wanted was to be wanted, and I was ready to attain that at any cost. I would live at Eva's. I would guzzle the chalky powdered protein until I no longer looked like a deformed and sickly bird. I had learned my lesson, and it had taken the cost of my self-respect and my heart to attain it.

This is the movie-montage portion of the journey where you see me running on the treadmill and pumping iron. Then you see me at the salon dying my hair. Then you see me gnawing at a raw head of kale like a tortoise and pounding protein shakes. I knew it wouldn't be easy, but it seemed I didn't have another choice. My heart had led me in the completely wrong direction. It was time to start thinking with my head.

124 Old Rabbit Club

☆ ☆ ☆ ☆ ☆

Category: Bars

Neighborhood: Greenwich Village

The Rabbit Club is the bar of my dreams.

It's the kind of place that I always dreamed existed before I ever moved to New York City. In an early premonition of my life, I pictured the dark, subterranean room filled with nothing but candlelight and a subtle red glow coming from an undetermined location. I knew I would someday find this bar, which served only beer and always seemed to be playing music that was completely in sync with whatever foul or joyous mood I was in. It is the greatest validation in life when you find the places that you just know you were meant to exist in. The same could be said of the people you choose to love. When it's right, at least.

I suppose I fit the bill when I poured myself into the hidden door that was just below street level on crowded Macdougal Street. Up above were the masses tripping over each other and their own paltry problems; they all had no idea what was going on below. As I opened the door, I was greeted by a nearly empty bar and the soft muffle of vintage garage punk music wafting through the dank air. It was perfect.

I couldn't imagine a place on earth that I would rather sit and drink beers with myself and my crushing disdain.

I had always feared it would come to this. I somewhat expected that the day would come where I would be sitting at a bar by myself pounding beer and listening to Patsy Cline crooning "Crazy." It was another bad day in a long line of bad days, and it had finally won me over to the dark side. I came to the Rabbit Club chasing a ghost, as I tended to do those days, and hoped that if I drank an entire large bottle of Rodenbach Grand Cru by myself, the specter of Him would materialize. I knew this was out of the question, because he was 3,000 miles away in Napa Valley spending the holidays with his family.

Weeks earlier, we had sat in the exact spot at the bar and shared a Rodenbach between us. The bartender with a heart of gold had kept feeding us beers and telling us how she could feel how palpably in love we were. He was holding onto my arm with one of his hands and clutching the glass of sour beer in the other. We swayed with the country music like we were wearing it as a costume, and the twang warmed us into a state of beer-glazed bliss. We laughed, told stories, laughed some more, and kissed as we fell into a buzz that I never wanted to go away. I was completely lost in Him, and his words and ideas wrapped around me like a blanket and soothed me into hysteric happiness.

It was another one of those places that I would never look at the same way again. Like the Temperance Fountain in Tompkins Square and Café Mogador on St. Mark's and so many other places I had come to claim as my favorite place on Earth, now the Rabbit Club belonged to Him, too. I would learn my lesson the next time I fell in love—keep some things to yourself. If I ever had a new favorite place to drink beer, I would go to it only by myself so that it could never be haunted by the utter sadness of losing one's heart. I just hadn't expected that if I showed Him my world and the things that I loved, he could potentially leave with it all. There I was again, ghostbusting and trying to uplift my spirits with nostalgia that didn't want to be remembered in the first place.

The thing that he never knew about me was that I desperately wanted to be Him. I wanted to be the one who didn't care, didn't want a future, or didn't want to be loyal. I wished that I could turn my heart on and off like a light switch, one minute having beers with me and kissing my neck and the next minute ready to walk out the door and onto the next. In a selfish fantasy, I began to wish that I, too, could haunt his favorite places in New York City. The only problem with that was he didn't have any places—they had all been mine. He was new and scared. Maybe that's the real reason he left me: to carve out his own places without an old "regular" like me getting in his way.

I feared that I would never make it to his "Rabbit Club" or his "Temperance Fountain." I'd never be important enough for Him to let me see the things in his life that brought him joy. Hell—he didn't even want to be associated with me on any social media sites: I wanted a partner and lover, and he wouldn't even friend me. Someday I'll laugh about this. I guess I just wanted too much. Being with Him was like drinking an entire bottle of the Grand Cru—one can't handle it all on their own without getting sick.

As I sat there and finished the gigantic beer by myself, I wondered what he was thinking all the way across the continent. I hoped he was in a happy place, like the Rabbit Club used to be my happy place. I hope our worlds weren't forever stained with our own ignorance and our own selfish folly. I went home—across the street—and threw up all of the expensive sour beer that I drank in a violent cacophony of tear-streaked gagging.

Tompkins Square Park
☆ ☆ ☆ ☆ ☆

Category: Parks
Neighborhoods: East Village, Alphabet City

Dear (Him),

The Temperance Fountain in Tompkins Square Park was built in 1888 by Henry D. Cogswell. He was a wealthy businessman and dentist from San Francisco. After living in New York for thirteen years, you would think I would have known more about this famous monument. Hell, there was even that one night I slept by it. It's one of those things for me—a place that I can't explain but am drawn to and almost magnetized by. Summer, winter, spring, and fall all find me there sitting in Tompkins Square and just staring at the thing. I can only imagine how many times I have sat there, sometimes with you, and meditated on the inscriptions on its sides: Temperance, Hope, Faith, and Charity.

I tossed the words around until they became divine, or perhaps a sign from the universe telling me that everything was going to be okay. I especially was drawn to the word "temperance." What did it mean? How was a bawdy peacock of a man like myself to learn the virtue of self-restraint? What would I learn if I learned to regulate myself and my locomotive heart?

It was finally revealed to me after doing some research that this Cogswell fellow was a total prude. The fountain itself was installed during a time in New York when the East Side was rampant with what Cogswell thought were derelicts. Much like today, everyone was running around all drunk and careening through their wild lives. Nothing much has changed since then. Perhaps the costumes. Cogswell wanted to preach the gospel of restraint and thought that installing a drinking fountain would provide clean water to the masses that most of the time opted for beer as their drink of choice. Imagine those times—no clean water so you had to resort to beer. Maybe Cogswell was doing the right thing, but he sounded like kind of a bummer to me.

Perhaps temperance was what I had needed. I think I learned a lot about restraint from you. I was on a fast train to nowhere before I met you, and I was totally happy being a hedonistic wild child with no goals and no hesitation. Being with you made me want to change, and that was one of the reasons why I loved you so much. You made me want to be a better person, and I was. In fact, I was the best version of myself that I had ever known. Certainly the happiest person I had ever been. I had hoped, foolishly, that maybe some of that temperance would rub off on you. The dictionary definition of temperance describes it as a virtue and refers to humility, self-restraint, and mercy. Each of these involves restraining some impulse, such as sexual desire, vanity, or anger. My, what a lovely thought it was that perhaps I could teach you how to do that. Perhaps if I could, we would be together. If I could teach you temperance, then we could be together forever and happily ever after.

Maybe it did sound like a total bummer. But what is wrong with not being the wild animal I thought I had wanted to be in my early 20s? I desperately needed temperance. My time had been wasted getting drunk and fucking anybody I saw fit. I've lived more than enough wild nights. I've drunk enough beer. I've fucked enough guys. I've had enough. All I wanted was for my life to go on and finally have some meaning. I wanted you. I wanted to be your champion, and I wanted to take care of you and make your life beautiful and fulfilling. I wanted to (attempt to) cook you dinner and keep you healthy in mind, body, and soul. I wanted to be your biggest fan, even when your ideas weren't so great. Most of all, I just wanted someone on my side. I know you have always felt incredibly lonely, and you may be surprised to find out that I have always felt very much the same. None of my so-called friends know the person that I really am, and it is completely my fault that I have put up the façade of an epic hedonistic mess. I let you see a side of me that no one gets to see, and that is the side that just wants to belong to someone completely. To hell with my freedom to do as I like—it was not good for me anyway.

I've always dreamed of leaving my mark on this city in some way. It has always terrified me that I'd just slip through the cracks and into obscurity. I wanted to write books that spoke of my most ardent passions and my lowest lows. I wanted people to be able to see that I WAS HERE. This is my city, and my fountain, and my memories. I will always return to the Temperance Fountain and think of myself and how I used to be. Now I will always think of you.

Never forget that you were here. Never forget that you came into my life and made me feel more in love than I have ever felt in my entire life.

The tile I commissioned to be made for you will be placed at the foot of the Temperance Fountain by the East Village Parks Conservancy. Although I had it made before Christmas, it won't be installed until the spring. I found this to be terribly fitting as the springtime was when I met you and you changed my life forever. The springtime symbolizes rebirth and the return of all of that beautiful whimsy that we used to revel in. My donation to the conservancy will see that flowers are planted in the spring so that all may enjoy them. It is with the most honest heart that I can say that all I want is to make this park, which has meant so much to me for so long, an even more beautiful place. I hope that when my flowers bloom, two young men who are freshly in love can look at them and feel the happiness that I once felt. I want to fix it. I want things to be beautiful again the way they were when I first fell in love with you.

Now you have a place here for the rest of your life. You are a part of this city. You will always be set in stone, both physically and metaphorically in my heart. Please take the time to come and visit this sacred place. Please come and just think about temperance and all that could have been if we had just had a little restraint. When you see the tulips next spring, know that I put them there for you. No matter how cold the winter gets, the spring will come, and the flowers will bloom. You meant so much to me. I'm so sorry you weren't ready.

I'll be visiting the fountain a lot, too, this spring, if this godforsaken winter ever ends. It brings me such joy to know that my love will be there set in stone forever. For as long as New York City exists, and even after we have passed from this world. I'm so glad I finally left my mark. This will be a constant reminder that I know the true meaning of love. This is my jellyfish tattoo, like the penny, and it can never be removed or forgotten. I promise I will be good and I will observe temperance. As you know, a promise is a promise.

I hope you like it. I know you were hoping for a new wallet or an iPad, and I suppose it's a little selfish of me to get you this, being as how it's kind of for me, too. I hope the weather is warm, and I find it so funny that we are both 3,000 miles away from what is now our real home. I pray that you are happy and that your mom is happy and that you feel better. I know your mom probably doesn't even know who I am, but please tell her that I want to thank her for taking care of you. I know how much she means to you. I hope the two of you can go to the Goodwill together and you can show her how it's really done. I would give anything to see that happen.

Merry Christmas, (Him). I will always miss you.

Chapter Five

I RETURNED TO CALIFORNIA AGAIN TO SPEND CHRISTMAS with my family. Although I had just been there after the Thanksgiving meltdown, I knew I had to be around my family for the holidays if I didn't want to lose my mind in Manhattan spending Christmas completely alone. I didn't have a choice. I just had to get out of New York and out of my own head.

My parents knew to handle me with the right amount of coddling. They had tried to lift my spirits the month prior by taking me on hikes in Malibu and making sure I was eating properly. Surely they had noticed that I was having a hard time feeding myself because of my new skeletal frame. Although I couldn't taste a thing, I forced my mother's amazing home-cooked meals down my throat and attempted to feign satisfaction.

Mom put up a record five Christmas trees in the house that year. There was a great big one in the vestibule and several small ones scattered throughout the other rooms. Cautiously, she asked me to come help her decorate them and put up the ornaments that had been mine from childhood. It was very clear that she was putting forth extra effort into making the house as festive as possible to try and lift my spirits. I grumbled and muttered from my post on the couch wrapped in blankets like a crazy person before burying my head in the cushions. Playing all around me was the meanest, cruelest, most sickening Christmas carols ever sang.

"I'll Be Home for Christmas"

"Last Christmas" (I gave you my heart, but the very next day you gave it away).

"All I Want for Christmas Is You"

Bah humbug, Mariah. Bah fucking humbug.

I watched local news and tried to eat as many cookies as I could force myself to eat. In between visits from my extended family and outings to the grocery store to stock up on tequila for the margaritas I was living on, I wrote. I sat at my laptop and began to write out the story of how I had come to the place I was now in. It felt like an exorcism, and as I recounted all of the time and places we had been together, I began to feel a lightness form in my heart.

These were the stories that would eventually come to smear the Internet with the tale of a love gone terribly wrong. I didn't know it at the time, but eventually these vignettes of heartbreak would be read by strangers all over the country and the world at large. Once I put these tales out into the great beyond of the world wide web, it didn't even occur to me that people might actually see them. What's more, people would respond.

I didn't even think that anyone in the world could ever relate to having their hearts broken as hard as mine had been. I thought that I was special—I was the only man in the world to have ever been wronged by that fat little Cupid asshole. When I started to post my stories on Yelp, I felt like a graffiti artist. I was tagging up a wall where people were trying to find a good cheeseburger with the musings of my innermost personal baggage. In time, people began to stumble upon the story. When in search of the best crème brûlée in the city, people began to stumble upon my "review" of the night my world came crashing down around me at the French Roast. Eventually, people would stumble across my broken heart while on a search for good pierogies and be directed to my review of Veselka.

After I returned home from my Christmas in California, things began to get a little strange. I had started to post my stories on Yelp regularly, and, to my surprise, I began to get responses from people. Being that my email address was listed on the homepage of my Yelp profile, I started to get emails from complete strangers from all over the world. As corny as it sounded, the Internet had made it possible for me to achieve a sense of community with a group of people whom I hadn't known even existed: The Community of The Heartbroken.

Every morning when I awoke and went to check my email, I would have emails sent to me from people who were dealing with the same exact problems I was dealing with. Well—perhaps not exactly the same, but at least similar. There was a heartbroken mother of two from somewhere in the Midwest who told me to hold on because it was going to get better. There was a man in Rome who told me that he knew exactly how I had felt because he had just gone through a terrible breakup himself. There was even a young woman in Manhattan who wrote me a letter that changed the course of my intent forever. I began to realize that my story wasn't special at all: heartbreak was a universal thing, and it happened (hopefully) to every person to ever live.

I thought about Irwin, the young woman who wrote to me from Manhattan. She was on the very same island I was on, somewhere out there in the maze of people and lives, and she felt the same way I did. Perhaps I had crossed her on the street. If it weren't for sharing my story with the Internet, I'd never have received an email from her that put my problems into very real perspective.

Part of her message read:

> My boyfriend of a year and a half (whom I met on OKCupid, of course) broke up with me two weeks ago out of the blue, and reading your words were so devastatingly on point.
>
> I've been alternating between wandering the city and buying myself absurdly lavish single dinners (book in hand), to weeping in my nail salon mid-pedicure on 1st and Ave A. Everywhere I go I'm reminded of him, of something we did together, of a place we ate or a time we spent, and I am so afraid there isn't a place in Manhattan left where my heart won't break, or I won't sadistically order his favorite meal to savor what was. I'm a girl broken, still in the ashes, and I'm not totally sure I'll ever be a phoenix.

Particularly this paragraph stopped me cold, as she quoted my own words back to me:

> 'I thought long and hard about the rut I was in, and why I was in it to begin with. I was downtrodden and broken, homesick, and ill at ease. I was bruised, and battered, and withering like a grape into a raisin, and this made me realize that all I ever wanted was . . .

someone to just do something. All I ever wanted was someone to say that they saw me and cared about me and wanted to help. This city chews boys like me up and spits them out every day, and without a little help from the rest of the world (friends, lovers, strangers on the street) it can be unbearably lonely.'

Just wanted to let you know you're not the only one. This weekend I held a woman I didn't know as she cried next to the napkins in the Five Guys on 55th. Her partner had said something that hurt her feelings, and she had gotten up from her table across from me, tears bulging out of her eyes, to go hide next to the concessions around the corner so their four kids wouldn't see.

I'm so lonely. I'm so devastatingly beaten up and broken and sad and missing the sunny South I came from and doubting I'll ever feel as happy or as in love as I was a month ago. A good friend of mine keeps telling me 'this is not forever.' I want to believe her, but it's hard.

Please don't feel pressured to respond. I'm sure you're being flooded by every lonely heart in the city! I just wanted to let you know I've got a fortune cookie slip I'll keep forever too. I see you. I care about you. And I'm not sure I can help, as I can't really help myself. But I want to anyway.

Sending you all the healing energy I can muster, Irwin

It knocked me off of my feet.

I couldn't believe that there were people out there who were as desperate and lonely as I was. I mean . . . I could believe it, if I really thought about it. When faced with such a situation, naturally all one could ever ask for is for someone to say "I see you. I care about you." This made me want to start an army. I wanted to march triumphantly down 5th Avenue with my army of heartbroken lepers hoisting big picket signs that read "Broken but Not Beaten" and chanting "We're here! We're heartbroken! We're getting used to it, although it's not easy and sometimes we want to crawl into a hole and die!"

Hearing that I was not alone in my pain gave me a burning desire to continue to tell my story. I wanted to capture every detail, every restaurant, and every memory that had brought me to the lonely place I resided in. I had found my way to tell my story in the strangest, most unassuming and abstract way possible. I continued to Yelp as my story continued, and I was hopeful that eventually the story would take a happy turn and see me fully recovered from my ground-zero status. I wanted to share with the world that maybe, just maybe, there was light at the end of the tunnel.

I continued to Yelp. It was all I knew how to do.

7A - CLOSED
☆ ☆ ☆ ☆ ☆

Categories: Bars, Burgers
Neighborhoods: East Village, Alphabet City

I think Joni Mitchell said it best when she sang, "Don't it always seem to go that you don't know what you got til it's gone? They paved paradise and put up a parking lot."

As real estate goes in New York City, they were always tearing down things that had been a place of consequence and putting up a big dumb bank or chain restaurant in its place. I had watched for almost fourteen years as the places I once held memorable were razed and replaced with inauthentic, boring dumps that you could find anywhere else in America. In a world where we are taught not to be afraid of change, sometimes it can be hard to realize that maybe it's all a bunch of bullshit. Maybe things should just stay the way they are, for fear of turning into something that could never think to compare to the original luster of its initial conception.

I had tried my hardest to make my relationship with Him something that would always be set in stone and impossible to replace. When I bought him a memorial tile that would be engraved in his honor and placed at the foot of the Temperance Fountain in Tompkins Square Park, I knew that it would be something that could never be torn down and turned into a CitiBank or Starbucks. It was just a little piece of stone, but it would be there forever, long after all of the East Village was turned into Middle America. In this regard, I would always have the memory of how ardently I had cared for Him. Despite that, everything else would change and perhaps that memory would be lost in the mire of "progress."

7A was closing down, and it was another one of those places that I had spent much of my youth in. Back when I first moved to New York, I had fancied myself to be the mayor of the gay East Village. Self-important and decked out in safety-pin laden rags and a rock-hard Mohawk haircut, I had poured myself into booths at 7A and gorged happily on gigantic salads and French fries. It was a place where I drank black coffees at three in the morning and mimosas at noon. It was always the place that came after a night out drinking where I could sit down and regain my bearings by sustaining myself with a delicious sandwich and try to return to the land of the conscious. I began to think about the time not long ago when I went there with Him, and we sat in a booth side by side and shared a meal as we curled up into each other. It can be so hard to sit across the table from someone you just want to live inside of. We were honestly attached at the hip.

As the couple across the room from us got up to leave after paying their bill, the woman stopped and interrupted our feeding frenzy. She said how happy we looked and that we were a perfect couple. She was right, you know. Back then we were both so happy, before all of the shit hit the fan. People like that woman used to stop us on the street wherever we went and tell us what a gorgeous couple we were—mostly because we were always smiling and laughing and basking in each other's general merriment. It was hard not to believe that we were destined to be together: if everyone else in the world knew it, then why shouldn't we?

It's all perspective, in the end. The glorious times in my youth that I spent avoiding my life's progression in a mire of beer and cheeseburgers at 7A were perhaps not the days of glory I seemed to remember. Maybe it was all just something that needed to be let go of, even if the future was such a scary and unforgiving place. Maybe the place deserved to be shut down and turned into a CitiBank. Even since when I had been there last, with Him, I had become a new person. The future—and change—was coming whether I liked it or not. People come and people go, and if it's not set in stone, then it will probably just rust and fade away. Who's to say this isn't the way it's supposed to be?

There comes a time when you just have to let go, and move forward. Nothing in this world lasts forever, and if it did, the world would probably be a lot less exciting. 7A should be burnt to the ground. Start from scratch. If it's going to be rebuilt as a Gap clothing store, then I hope it is the best Gap clothing store that has ever been built. I had come so far from my days as a rebel youth meandering through the East Village and crushing beers at dumps like 7A with boys who never even cared about me. I had even come so far from Him as it finally clicked in my head that I would never be enough for Him.

New York is a mistress of disguise, and just when you think you get comfortable with something (a restaurant, an apartment, a man) it changes right before your eyes. In order to keep up with her, you have to keep the pace yourself or get trampled and left in the dust. It's evolution. It's survival of the fittest. It's Darwinism of the Heart.

I would change. I would not be kept in the past. And hopefully I wouldn't be transformed into a shitty Starbucks version of myself just because the world wanted it that way.

Susanna Pizzeria
☆ ☆ ☆ ☆ ☆

Categories: Italian, Pizza
Neighborhood: Greenwich Village

If one thing is true, it is that there is absolutely no shortage of pizza in the West Village. There's pizza of every single type that can please every sort of person: thin cracker-like crust, deep dish, rustic Italian style, cheap dollar slices, whole pies, brick oven, and a million others. I've had them all. Much like anything else in life, I like to give everyone a chance. Life is too short not to taste every flavor available, and it would be a shame to miss out on the perfect slice just because you always go to the same pizzeria.

In this way, men in New York City are like pizza. I have tasted each and every one of them. There is certainly no shortage of every flavor of bachelor you could ever imagine here. There's junk food men that cost a dollar and taste the same, men who are artisanal and elitist, and men who taste good but leave you with a terribly upset stomach shortly after indulging in them. If I were a pizza, I have to assume that I would be a pie from Susanna Pizzeria.

This is sad, because I've always considered this place to be a hopeless loner that would never last on the Manhattan pizza circuit for long.

It's always empty, and it just has this kind of sad, desperate vibe about it.

Breaking up can be absolute murder on your self-esteem. Especially when your ex is a blood-hungry emotional vampire that can only be sustained with your tears and completely sucking you dry of your self-respect. That being said, I always felt sorry for Susanna. I felt like it deserved a chance. As I walked around my neighborhood feeling like the most single person in all of Manhattan, my heart nearly broke when I passed this pizzeria and saw that it was still completely empty. So I went in. "You and I are going to be okay, Susanna," I said to myself. Then I panicked because I realized I had become the type of person who talks to themselves in public. "Shut up and order a pizza," I said. Thank God there was no one around to see me convincing myself that I wasn't about to totally unravel.

This had become my new life, and it startled me. I hate going to dinner by myself. I always have such a hard time because I feel like I should be doing something, so my first impulse is to get on my stupid phone. Then I try to avoid that because I hate being the type of person who has to always be on their phone. I harden my resolve and just sit and look around, almost as if to say, "Look, I'm fine just existing in the moment and not being connected to the whole of the world." It's a complete lie, and it makes me uncomfortable, but I force the restraint on myself anyway. I just sat and surveyed the empty room and patiently waited for my pizza.

Immediately, I began to wish that I were at home, lying in bed scratching myself and watching crappy television, eating a pizza from Domino's.

I felt like a fool sitting there in the empty room, even though I knew that it was all just an act of kindness to make Susanna feel not so hopeless and alone. Selfish old me, I just wanted to eat my pizza in shame behind closed doors. Because eating pizza alone is sad. A slice—sure, that's fine and acceptable for the bachelor on the go. But a whole pizza? It just didn't feel right.

So I ate the whole thing as fast as I could. This was not a hard task; I had not eaten a single thing all day and I was starving. Plus, it wasn't even that large. Plus, it was freakin' delicious. Or was it? Was I just convincing myself that this pizza was indeed worthy of love, or was I genuinely satisfied with it despite all of the other pizza options available to me but a stone's throw away? Now it had become personal—if I didn't eat this entire pizza by myself, then I was letting Susanna down. She didn't deserve that. She deserved a chance to stand up to all of the other pizza people on the block. And by God, the pizza *was* actually good!

Men and pizza. Pizza and Men. Both will ruin your life if you have too much of them. They'll make you fat and slow you down. They always seem like a good idea, but sometimes you really just need a salad. I'm glad I gave Susanna Pizzeria a try, if only to prove to myself that I was going to be okay in a sea of other options, even if the other options were actually better. I decimated that pizza, left the waiter a 50 percent tip, and walked home. Was my mind blown? No. But I walked home proud, knowing that I was still going to give everything a chance. I was still looking for the perfect pie and the perfect man and maybe neither of those things even existed, but I was going to take the virtuous road to get to either of them anyhow. It's New York City. We're famous for this stuff, but people get so caught up in the "Famous Ray's" and the "Famous Ben's" and famous whatever that they overlook the little guy.

I'm still looking for the perfect pie. I think I'm on the right track.

Tue Thai Restaurant

☆ ☆ ☆ ☆ ☆

Category: Thai
Neighborhood: West Village

I was changing. I couldn't help it.

I thought it was something I could stifle, and that it would just go away if I ignored it long enough. Much like many of my problems in life, I had always believed that if I just pretended it wasn't there, then it would just work itself out in the end, and as a result I would be "changed." The thing is, I'd have happily stayed the same person I'd always been if not for my broken heart. In a corny, Hallmark way, it's exactly as they say: it's always darkest before the dawn.

I thought long and hard about the rut I was in and why I was in it to begin with. I was downtrodden and broken, homesick and ill at ease. I was bruised, and battered, and withering like a grape into a raisin, and this made me realize that all I ever wanted was . . . someone to just do something. All I ever wanted was someone to say that they saw me, and cared about me, and wanted to help. This city chews boys like me up and spits them out every day, and without a little help from the rest of the world (friends, lovers, strangers on the street), it can be unbearably lonely. I wanted to help myself out, and I realized that the only way I could do this was to start on the outside: help someone else.

I painted and I wrote and I filled myself with delicious health food. I took walks and I saw movies and I sat in the park and felt the sunshine on my skin. It was all good and healing, yes, but I wanted more. I wanted to take this feeling that I had to the next level, and hoped that I could save a poor wretch like me from feeling like they were all alone.

What is it with gays and Thai food? I've always been a fan of a cheap lunch special, and Thai food is always the most affordable and somewhat healthy option a guy can choose. Chelsea and Hell's Kitchen are littered with them, one after another, and each one is basically the same. It's as if there could be one long kitchen running the span of the avenue behind the walls that just has several little outlets. Regardless, it's just always what I want. They know what they're doing, and I take myself to lunch at several Thai places on a weekly basis.

My favorite is Tue on Greenwich. This part of the neighborhood speaks to me on so many levels, and it always just feels special for some reason. I go there the most, and these days I go alone. I sat there today, without a book for a change, and just watched my surroundings. As I happily took to my curry, I noticed a young man walk in and sit down by himself. He was a waif of a thing carrying a big book bag, and he was wearing a shirt from Trader Joe's. I figured he must be a bag boy either on break or on his way to work. The young man was obviously looking in my direction from across the way, not in a sexual way, but in a way that conveyed "Hey, I'm here, too. I'm having lunch by myself, and that's okay."

I watched as he tore into his pad thai like he hadn't eaten in weeks. Between bites, he would look at his phone, smile, and then resume his binging. I wondered if people ever looked at me when I was out to lunch with myself. I wondered if anyone ever looked at me and wondered how my day was going.

On my way out, I stopped at the host stand and spoke to the young woman who was polishing menus. I explained to her the best I could that I wanted to buy the young man in the corner his lunch. She didn't comprehend at first, so I told her the honest truth: I just wanted to do something nice for someone today. She looked at me as if I were crazy. It wasn't like I was buying a stranger a Porsche or anything—I just wanted this young man to know that there was kindness in this cold, hard, unforgiving city. If I could make someone happy today, then I knew that I was going to be okay. The best feeling in life is knowing that your destiny is one hundred percent in your own hands. I knew that I could find my own joy by bringing joy to someone else, even if it was only over cheap pad thai. I'd made it my mission to save myself by being the best person I could be. There are so many things I am not: wealthy, fit, selfish, vain. I had to focus on the things that I did have, and that was the ability to make others know that they are loved. It's not much, but it's what I have to work with. I may never be a wildly successful author, and I may never have the body of a Greek god, but I will always, always have the ability to make someone smile.

I paid my check and the stranger's, and then walked out the door without even turning to look back. I felt light as a feather, and I floated my way back home feeling like the happiest boy in all of Greenwich Village.

Sundaes and Cones

☆ ☆ ☆ ☆ ☆

Category: Ice Cream & Frozen Yogurt
Neighborhood: East Village

As the snow came down, I stopped in the middle of Saint Mark's Place—yes, the middle of the street—and wondered what I was doing.

The cars at the stoplight stared right at me as if they were the bulls in Pamplona bracing to take off and hunt me down like prey. The term "deer in the headlights" suddenly became apparent and frightfully true. As yellow turned to red on the crossing signal, I scurried my way to the other side as the cabs sped forward, honking their horns and swiftly swerving to avoid my untimely demise. Safely on the other side, I exhaled and continued on my way to Sundaes and Cones.

I began to wonder how I had become the type of person that goes out to have ice cream by himself for breakfast. In the snow. On a weekday.

I guess I was just feeling sorry for myself. In the wake of being the happiest person in the world last summer, I had let myself slide into a creature of pure impulse. If anything could make me feel as slightly happy as I did back then, then I pined and begged for it. I used to go to Sundaes and Cones with Him, and it was an almost spiritual experience. I remember how I ravaged the cup of taro root ice cream with Him sitting so close by my side on the bench outside. Our knees were touching, and even though it was starting to get cold outside, I felt warm with content and the heat coming off of his body, which I loved every nook and cranny of. This also conjured images of the Christmas card he gave to me over a late-night date at Coppelia before I left for California. On its front was a picture of two ice-cream cones making out with each other; the inside read "You Make Me Melt." Then, in his child-like handwriting, "The fact that we're still trying to make it work speaks volumes of how True this love is . . . I'm committed to moving forward with you in a loving, caring, and honest way."

And yet today, he was nowhere to be seen. Just another memory that I relished and hoped I could revive, like I was giving it CPR, by ordering both Him and myself ice cream. I ate my cup of taro root, and his just sat there melting. I prayed that at any moment he would walk through the door, and there it would be just waiting for Him. I knew it was foolish as I did it, but it didn't matter.

I stood at the display case and stared intensely at all of the beautiful ice cream cakes. They were so artfully minimalist, and beautiful, and I thought about how easy it would be for me to eat one in its entirety. There was one in particular that stood out to me that was different from the rest. It was a small cake with green frosting that was made to look like grass, with patches of little green icing that looked like shrubbery. Dotted among the shrubs were little piles of brown fondant shaped like piles of poop. At this, I laughed.

I wanted this cake with all of my heart and wished that someone would buy it for me. I wanted this cake to be my wedding cake because it made all of the sense in the world. Life is shitty. Shit happens. Shit hits the fan, but thank God there is ice cream cake in the world. My relationship with Him was the absolute embodiment of this very cake sitting in the case before me. It looked very shitty—it really did. It was covered in poop, and probably not many people would consider it to be something worth having. But I knew in my heart that it wasn't really poop—it was frosting. It was all just freaking frosting. Beneath that shitty visage that the world was tricked into seeing was ice cream. And cake. And I love ice cream and cake.

My birthday is in August, but I wouldn't want this cake for my birthday. I really and truly believed that I wanted this to be the cake that the man of my dreams would let me have at our wedding. My parents would scoff, his would recoil in disgust, and all of our friends would think that we were the tackiest people in the world for turning the wedding our community fought so hard to make legal into a running poop joke. My grandmother would think it perverse and faint on the spot. But I would get it, and it wouldn't be a joke to me.

Love is the hardest thing in the world to get right. It is not a piece of cake. It's no walk in the park, and it hurts so badly sometimes that you can't imagine going on without it. It's shitty. It's ugly, and its beautiful, and it's more important that anything in the world. I wanted, so, so badly to eat this shit.

As I sat in the window with my two ice creams, I watched as the snow began to slowly subside. For a moment, the sky was filled with flurries softly floating about, but the clouds dispersed and made way for a brilliantly sunny sky. Finishing my cup of ice cream to the point of nearly licking the little cup clean, I looked over at the untouched scoop of cookies and cream that I had bought for Him. I had half a mind to take to it too and eat every last bite, but I suddenly thought better of myself. I threw it in the trash.

Cafeteria

☆ ☆ ☆ ☆ ☆

Categories: American (New), Southern, Breakfast & Brunch, Diners
Neighborhood: Chelsea

"You think I won't do it?" I asked as I looked up at him from my beer. I was surely a bit cockeyed, and I'd never had the best poker face to begin with. Bravado has, more often than not, been the villain that has forced me into many a complicated situation. I was suddenly terrified that he was going to call me out.

"No way," he said, wearing a wicked grin. He'd known me for too long, and he knew exactly how to press all of my buttons.

"Fine," I responded defiantly as I grabbed a menu off the bar. "I've done it before and I can do it again. Just because I've not done something in the past does not make me a slave to it for the rest of my life. I'm a new man. I'm reborn. I'm the phoenix from the ashes!" I began to feel my adrenaline pumping in my chest. Me and my big mouth.

It's funny the way life works. I'd been a regular at Cafeteria since its heyday back in the early 2000s, and here I was sitting at the bar with a man I'd once courted romantically in this very room. This was a lover from centuries before Him. The setting had changed, and Cafeteria was no longer the feral nightlife monstrosity it once was, but then again, neither was I. I sat with my ex, who was now no more than a friend, and now felt oddly familiar with my old self. I'd not seen this brazen version of myself in what seemed like forever.

"Biscuits and gravy," I shouted to the bartender, "with scrambled eggs and cheese, please!"

We were back on the whole "egg thing" again. I had successfully managed to go through thirty-one years of my life without eating an egg, and I was, for some reason, proud of it. It was almost like a badge that I wore, and it could almost be seen as a character trait. It was just something I didn't do. This was important, because as an artist and a generally free spirit, there was not a lot that I could say no to in this world.

Although I would like to chalk it up to some long-winded defense about how inherently disgusting the egg is, it's only been fear that has kept me from eating them. Fear is the catalyst for stagnation, and stagnation had become something that I was not willing to tolerate in my new way of life. It was only a few months ago that I had attempted to eat an egg. I was in a fight with Him over something inane, I'm sure. He was mad, and I didn't know at the time how to convince Him that I'd do absolutely anything in the entire world to let Him know how much I loved Him. So I went to the bodega and bought half a dozen eggs.

I scrambled them to the best of my ability, being as how I am neither a good cook nor do I know especially how to prepare an egg. With shaky hands, I took a forkful of the yellow mess, and with my other hand steadied my phone to capture a video of me shoveling it into my mouth as proof. My stomach began to rise into my throat, and I felt as if I would vomit at any moment. But I took the hefty forkful and chewed it until I could swallow it. This was perhaps one of the things I loved most about my time with Him: it challenged me and made me face my fears. Even if it was for all the wrong reasons.

Eleanor Roosevelt once said, "Do one thing every day that scares you."

This time would be different. I didn't want to eat eggs to save my ass or get me out of a hairy situation. I wanted to do it for myself. I wanted to show myself that although it felt like it wouldn't at times, my life would go on. There is nothing that we as humans can't accomplish if we put our minds to it, even if it is such a little thing. Sometimes it's the little things that come across as our greatest fears, and it is up to us to put an end to those fears, because no one else can. It was a small battle, and yet it felt like a war: me vs. the egg. Luckily for me, I had new artillery: hope.

"I'm gonna do it."

"Fine. Do it," he said.

"I am. I really, really am. Screw this. I'm not afraid. There's nothing to be afraid of," I said, and even as I said it began to quiver with anxiety. The breakfast stared a hole right through my soul and spoke to me of greater fears to overcome.

Baby steps. I could take baby steps, and soon I would live a life without fear. Fear of eggs. Fear of failure. Fear of being alone. I could conquer them all if I could just . . . get myself . . . to take . . . the first bite.

I closed my eyes and took a heaping bite.

Within a matter of minutes, I had cleared the plate. I dropped my fork with a clang on the bar and let my arms hang dumbfounded at my sides. I had done it. I was officially the bravest man in all of Manhattan. What mattered the most was not that I had done it to begin with, but that I had done it for myself. At the end of the day, I didn't die. I didn't vomit or cringe or wince at the wickedness of the egg. I had always believed that the world would cease to orbit once I finally overcame my fear. Truly, it made me stronger, and I could feel my blood pumping in my veins and a smile begin to streak its way across my face. I began my life as sunny-side up.

Dean & DeLuca

☆ ☆ ☆ ☆ ☆

Categories: Caterers, Specialty Food
Neighborhood: SoHo

As I walked through Dean & Deluca, I felt a wave of pure green envy begin to pummel me. Let's not call it green—let's call it "viridian." Somewhere between green and blue.

I was teeming with jealousy, as I usually was when I went into places like this. I remembered that Dean & Deluca was one of the first places I ever went to get a coffee when I first visited New York City as a teenager. I was poor at the time, with little more than pocket change and a duffle bag full of crumpled tee shirts, paintbrushes, and hopes. It was a classic Manhattan love story. Most of us have lived it in some capacity, and it's those first glances into a much larger world that shape us into the driven and relentless people we are today. I saw the well-to-do people of SoHo decked out in their all-black ensemble, drinking coffee and spending more money than I had to my name on organic produce and chic bottles of water. I was terrified, and yet I wanted so, so badly to fit in.

I didn't know how to go about it, but I knew I wanted into the club. My stomach grumbled hungrily, as I'd not much money to afford food, and I watched as all of the people chatted casually over sushi on the eating counters by the front door. Everyone was smiling, and I felt the monster beginning to grow inside of me: jealousy. It's been a constant question in my life, relevant in many ways: why can't it be me?

Today, as a grown man who has somewhat found his way in the world, I revisited Dean & Deluca. Although I still remembered first setting foot inside the brightly lit and bustling room as a teenager, I suddenly felt like I had finally become one of the lucky ones who got to enjoy it the way it was intended to be enjoyed. I pushed my way inside, shoulder-checking my way to the produce aisle. I had no need or want of produce; I didn't even have the desire to eat. That which I had once coveted seemed no longer desirable. It's a tale as old as time: be careful what you wish for.

My cravings had changed over the years, and my palate had sophisticated. The things that I wanted seemed more important than that initial hunger I once had. Although I'd no desire for expensive pastries and designer coffee, the Green Eyed Monster still nagged at my coattails. Even though I'd gotten everything I'd ever wanted, I'd still be jealous of Him.

I'd almost forgotten the way he had smelled by now. Or the way his voice sounded. But there were certainly some things that I'd not been able to shake. I walked around the produce aisle, touching all the fruit like a crazy person. The smooth skin of each watermelon, his forehead; the slightest dusting of fur on a peach, his butt. I knew in my heart that he had already forgotten the way my breath smelled in the morning, or the way that my lips felt on the back of his neck as I woke Him from his deep sleeping. He'd already found another man, and probably had come to love the little things about him that I once did that stirred a fire in Him.

Jealousy is the hardest battle to fight, especially when it is purely one-sided. I had craved Him endlessly, and yet he had found another. I had become the man I'd always dreamed and found a job, my niche, a fulfilling life. I had become the man I had once seen shopping in Dean & Deluca that I thought was the pinnacle of success, but I was still lonely.

Moving slowly from the produce department with one foot in front of the other, I found myself staring at a case full of gorgeous pastries. My eyes locked on a pile of the most beautiful almond croissants I'd ever seen. Instantly, I was taken back to the morning walks we used to take and the almond croissants we had shared while walking up Lafayette, which had somehow or another become the most traveled street in our day to day. He'd take massive bites and wind up with powdered sugar and big flakes of dough stuck in his dark red facial hair. With my free hand not clutching a cup of coffee, I'd reach up to dust him out, and he'd smile at me. I wondered if he shared croissants with his new lover. I wondered if they tasted even better than the ones with me.

I began to realize that everyone in Dean & Deluca was not the successful and impenetrable type that I had once pegged them for. We were all lost. It's just that some of us could afford designer baguettes and artisanal cheese. The only difference between my younger self and my current self was a better outfit and more money in my pocket.

I stopped to look at myself in the reflection of the glass door on the way out. Decked in all black, leather, and smelling of expensive cologne, I was something I'd never imagined. I thought this was what he had wanted.

Enough was not enough.

Chapter Six

WE DROVE TO MONTAUK in the middle of the night. I don't remember how or why; I tended to block out the unimportant logistics of our history. What I did remember was this: the freezing air blowing through my hair and chilling me to the bone beneath that shaggy Ralph Lauren sweater that we would henceforth refer to as "the Montauk sweater."

We had rented a convertible, because why not. We had pillaged his favorite store, the Goodwill on 9th Street, for used CDs to curate the perfect soundtrack for our spur-of-the-moment escape from the City. "Jagged Little Pill" was playing as we sped away from our hum-drum, typical little lives in Manhattan. Looking back, to think that we were bored with our day to day in the biggest and most exciting city in the world was foolish—but it spoke volumes of his general feeling toward life in general. He had always wanted more.

We went to Montauk simply because we could. I made a phone call to a woman I used to work with, completely out of the blue, and asked her if we could come and stay with her. She had gone to Montauk for the summer to work, and now that the summer was coming to an end, most of the inhabitants of the town were returning to Manhattan. The conversation was quick, and she didn't ask any questions. She just said that all of her flat mates had already left and she had the house all to herself, and that we were more than welcome to stay. So we went.

My adrenaline spiked as we sped off into the night on an impromptu adventure to a place neither of us had been before. So much of our life in Manhattan had been curated by me—I had lived there for over a decade and was always taking Him to somewhere I had discovered on my own. I was sure it probably stressed Him out that everywhere we went together was a direct result of my own familiarity with a city I had been in a relationship with that was well in its prime. On this night, however, he was driving me in that silver Mustang to a place I had never known. Because I had moved to New York at such a young age, I had never driven a car before. He took the wheel and held my hand the whole way as we drove.

We arrived at the house, a cozy little surf shack with surfboards hanging from the ceiling and a roaring fireplace going at full-blast, at around midnight. Our hostess, whom I affectionately referred to as "Aunt Sandy," was well into a very large bottle of cheap Pinot Grigio. He was having one of his regular stints of not drinking, so I too declined her offer to share the wine with her. We sat on the floor by the fire and caught up on chit-chat—most of what I contributed involved my current state of joy in having the company of Him. The whole thing felt surreal. It was as if my entire being had been electrified with the strange sensation of unfamiliarity with my surrounding and my general being.

Aunt Sandy enthusiastically decided that we should go to the beach. It was the middle of the night, and the wind was picking up, but no one seemed to care. In the spirit of adventure, I just looked over at Him and shrugged my shoulders and smiled. Again—why not?

It was apparent that Aunt Sandy was tipsy as we piled into her rickety old Jeep that didn't have any windows and seemed held together by faith. She ripped through the empty streets on our way to the beach, and we held on for dear life, occasionally gripping each other's hands as we turned sharp corners and gritted our teeth. In a matter of minutes, we pulled up to a pitch-black and deserted stretch of seaside.

Up by the water, the air was freezing. I wrapped the Montauk sweater around me, and he clung to my arm as we trod through the dunes to come to a sparse place with nothing but the wind and the light of a million stars surrounding us. The three of us lay down on the sand and stared up into the night sky, which was unfamiliar to the one I had been used to staring at back home in Manhattan. Unlike the City sky, this one was filled with stars. I had forgotten about the existence of stars, and, like many things I had come to take for granted, being with Him had brought them back into the forefront of my being. I sidled up close to Him for warmth, and he crawled up into the nook of my arm.

Shooting stars were everywhere. I made wishes for each one I saw. The first wish I made: please let me stay like this forever—never let this feeling end. It was a corny and utterly predictable whirlwind of romanticism, but my heart felt instantaneously so swollen in my chest that it threatened to burst. I felt like I could defy gravity and fall upward into the endless darkness and happily float out into nothing. He was my anchor, and his weight kept me pinned to the sand.

We barely slept that night. There was something propelling us out into this strange new world that couldn't let us be. We got up before the sunrise and went out to explore. Somehow we wound up back on the beach, and it was still deserted as far as the eye could see—nothing but miles of pristine sand and a faint orange light that was the sun beginning to rise. We walked on the beach hand in hand for a very long time until we eventually came upon an empty lifeguard tower. I dropped his hand and ran up to the tower, and although it did not have a ladder, I scaled it with ease.

He was afraid of heights—one of his many phobias that seemed so silly coming from a man that was so wild and filled with reckless bravado. He stood at the foot of the tower and paced repeating his common mantra of "I can't." I just nudged Him on, as usual, telling Him that it was okay and that I would help Him. I extended my arm, and he eventually, begrudgingly, took it, and I hoisted Him up to join me. Once he had settled in with me high atop the tower, he wrapped his arms around my arm and burrowed his head into my neck. His breath was noticeably warm amidst the cold morning air that was wrapped around us, and I felt it hit me and stay moist as he planted a series of small kisses on my neck.

I don't remember the exact conversation we had that morning on the lifeguard tower. I do remember the gist of it, though. It had to do with both of us realizing that this feeling we were sharing—this sunrise, this beach, this symbiotic warmth—could possibly last forever.

He said he had never felt so alive, and I couldn't help but agree. We existed in that moment and became frozen in time. This minute, this second, this place, and this sunrise were all becoming monuments in my memory of what I would keep from my time with Him.

We always used to play those silly scratch-off lottery tickets whenever we came across them in bodegas because being together made us feel lucky. We were lucky to have found each other, and he would say stupid things like, "I can't believe they made *two* of us." Win or lose, it didn't matter. We probably spent hundreds of dollars playing those dumb little things. To some, that would probably matter, but to me, it was a priceless purchase of time that I bought to spend with Him— giddy and hopeful at hitting a jackpot, which I felt I had already won. Truthfully, we never really "won" much more than a few dollars here and there, but the laughs we shared as a result were priceless.

The real treasure of my time spent with Him was not the epic sunrises or adventures out of town or shooting stars or lottery prizes. It was not the grand gestures that I built in attempts to keep Him even as he was pulling away from me over and over again. I had orchestrated a romance that I had been anticipating since the minute I came to New York. I had built a platform for this love and was spellbound as he took my carefully laid notion of love and rearranged it from the floor up.

This was where it all fell apart and the mythology of Us started to crumble from the inside out. We based our love on a series of cinematic cityscapes and sunsets and shooting stars and were left hollow by the day-to-day realness of what it meant to be in a "normal" relationship. Although I wanted to believe it could always be that way—almond croissants and fireworks and fireflies in the bushes while we kissed in the park—there was a stake that was set that made Him terrified of the commonplace. I felt that if I wasn't providing a pristine view from the top of a theoretical ferris wheel for Him, he would stray and look for another. And the truth was that I was absolutely right.

The many earthly splendors of New York made it easy to captivate his attention most of the time, but I knew that it just fueled his thirst for more. It's a city with a million different flavors and limitless possibilities—how was a man with his hunger for life not to taste them all? Such are the curses of our time. The world was now at our fingertips with the click of a button, the flash of a computer screen, or a simple head tilt from which to avert your gaze from your own reality. With so much world and so little me, it was impossible to assume that I was to be his endgame. After Montauk and Paris and Fourth of July and Central Park and Minetta Lane and the first snow and the last days of summer, there was just me—sitting in my small and quiet room up there on the fifth floor in my pajamas, waiting for the simple reality of *me* to be enough for Him.

Murray's Cheese Shop
☆ ☆ ☆ ☆ ☆

Category: Cheese Shops
Neighborhood: West Village

What I lack in common sense, I make up for in cheese knowledge.

I am the king of the dinner party cheese board. When I go into Murray's Cheese Shop, I go hard. I have a formula that I attend to, and it usually leads me to having a full-blown meal of free samples as I pick out the perfect New World–style aged manchego. The cheese mongers sigh and roll their eyes as they turn away from the counter as I contest the sharpness of their suggested Gouda that doesn't cut it for me. For someone as conflicted about every move I make in the world, I have a curt sense of steadfastness when it comes to my taste in triple crème.

One of my best friends was throwing a dinner party in Hell's Kitchen, and I arrived with a big bag of cheese in hand like I always did. She had lit every candle in her apartment, which looked a lot like the Mad Tea Party by way of Martha Stewart Living. Women who prefer the company of other women can be so heartwarming at times—the candles and the twinkly Christmas lights and the teacups everywhere made me weak in the knees. The soft jazz spoke to my soul. I knew it was inevitable that at some point we would do a group reading of passages printed out from online about the current moon cycle. Outside the second floor window it hung, bulbous and full.

Some days were better than others. This day was not one of them. I recalled a poem that I had read at a roundtable poetry reading at one of the last dinner parties she had thrown. It was by Marge Piercy, and the real kicker of it was the subtle synchronicities of the words "I went visiting, I ate meals, I sat in front of television and movie screens eyes glazed over like ponds just freezing opaque." I sat there amidst the festive chit-chat that these kinds of dinner parties tended to produce and stared at nothing. I spoke words but didn't feel them coming out of my mouth or even know their meaning. I was there, but I was not present.

As we sat around the table, I began by leading a prayer. We all held hands and closed our eyes and bowed our heads. Suddenly I felt like my dad, the big public speaker that I never really was. Prayer was not something I indulged in regularly, but it just seemed like the right thing to do at the time. It was a room full of artist types and the spiritually wayward, but I guess it was more about me just needing to do something for myself.

As much as I hated it, I'd fallen into a way of making everything come back to me somehow. In truth, I was sick of talking about myself and my stupid heart, so after the prayer I sat there at the table in complete silence. My friends told stories; I feigned laughter occasionally and nervously played with the rose petals that decorated the dinner table. Every time there was a lull in the conversation, I took a petal into my hands and played with it anxiously. I pressed them between my fingers under the table and rubbed them until their moisture began to seep out. Soon they became fragrant mush in my hands, and I didn't notice it initially, but by the time dinner was over there was a big pile of macerated rose sitting next to my untouched fork.

I wondered when I would just let it all go and allow myself to learn that this was all a vicious cycle of insanity. People changed, or so I wanted to believe, because I myself had become a completely different person than I was back in the day with Him. Maybe it was just my way, and not everyone wanted to change for the better. I couldn't press my path and my impression on Him, and I probably never would. But he still stuck there in my mind, and I wished that there was something I could say or do to make things otherwise. As he was out there somewhere in the city under the same fat moon hunting for new men and new conquests, I sat silently at a dinner table making an unintentionally perfumed mess and taking breaks from dinner to hide in the coat closet and cry.

It was just where I ended up. My friends had to have taken notice, for I kept returning to the table with my face like a puffer fish and my eyes swollen and red. They knew better than to say anything. We were all sick of talking about it. It had to just go away. As I curled up in a pile of coats on the floor of the closet, I tried my best to stifle the noises that were coming out of my body. I had to keep composed. I had to pull it together. I had to realize that it was just one bad day in the string of many good ones. He'd never go away completely, and surely there would be days when I couldn't shake that old feeling.

I emerged from the closet and walked slowly over to the spread of food laid out over by the kitchen. Duncan told a joke, and everyone laughed.

Sarah screamed her over-the-top yelp of jubilation. Miguel shoved cake in his mouth as Amanda put her arm around him.

Me? I went straight for the cheese. I pulled at the Morbier with my fingers. They were stained bright red from the roses, and I hadn't even noticed that I looked like I had committed a violent crime.

Happy Taco Burrito

☆ ☆ ☆ ☆ ☆

Categories: Tex-Mex, Mexican
Neighborhood: Greenwich Village

I had to look at it scientifically because if I chose to look at it any other way, I'd surely crumble. Steadfast in my way and certain of my choices, I grappled every day trying to wrap my head around whether or not the disintegration of my love life was because of lack of want or loss of need. Scientifically, I mused on the five steps of loss: denial/isolation, anger, bargaining, depression, and acceptance. Science is science, and there is little contesting that. In practice, I just ate—everything I could get my hands on.

Isolation had not been a problem at all, and I whizzed right past that one like I'd been doing it my whole life. He was nowhere to be seen, so I just rolled around on the floor of my apartment listening to PJ Harvey and moaning like a wounded yak. The denial part was a little trickier, as I truly believed that there was no way that he would actually want to give up even after the world came to a crashing halt—I hadn't wanted to, so why would he? I began to bargain, reasoning that if I went to the gym and ate a healthy diet of quinoa and feasted upon my longing, then I would have the body he found desirable and he'd have no need for others. This notion depressed me because all it reminded me of was the burgers we used to share at the Spotted Pig or the epic BBQ at Mighty Quinn's we would gorge on. Moderation was never our forte.

This all had to cumulate in depression eventually, and by January, I was knee-deep. It was like swimming in molasses, and it clung to every fiber of my being. A life in slow motion, coupled with one of the most devastating winters I'd seen in all my fourteen years as a New Yorker, had its grip on me and didn't want to let go. It was almost comical. I'd peek my head from under the covers some mornings to see snow falling (again) beyond my window . . . I'd just laugh. I'd stretch my arm out to his side of the bed, which was empty as usual, and feel for Him as if by some miracle he'd have snuck in in the middle of the night and crawled in with me. Mornings were the hardest, and I dwelled and I dwelled upon the possibility that he was waking up with someone else not a mile away on this cursed island. I'd look at the snow and grimace as if to say "you've got to be kidding me."

My stomach hadn't been the same since he left. I'd stopped eating altogether for a while, which only made my hunger that much more devastating when it got to the point that I could no longer live without food. So I ate everything in quantities so massive that the bags containing my delivered food contained enough cutlery to feed a family of six. Presumptuous bastards.

For a while, I tried to forget about the beautiful life I'd carved out with Him. I denied all of the decadent dinners at chic downtown hot spots and the romantic candlelit kisses in dark banquettes swathed in old leather. I denied holding his hand under tables of Manhattan's finest and cursed the thought that he was probably out there still sipping champagne at Carbonne or slurping escargot at Pastis.

I sat on my couch in my underwear and ate Happy Taco Burrito.

I can't say that it was good, because taste and enjoyment had no longer become priorities. I was solely eating to survive. And because it filled the hole. I can't say that it was bad because everything tasted like mulch, and I wasn't even sure if I still had the ability to enjoy things. All I knew was that there was a lot of it—and if I couldn't have quality, then I would settle for quantity. If only I had the audacity like he did to feel this way about men.

Tacos and nachos and burritos, oh my! I decimated them at such speed that I felt like the hotdog-eating king of Coney, Kobayashi, whose claim to fame was his iron stomach and his gaping jaw. I, too, had become a speed eater to keep up with Him and his eating habits that he must have developed as a result of his time in the military. Salsa spattered the table like a Jackson Pollack painting, and a ball of napkins formed at my side about six inches deep.

Much like anything in my life, metaphor was never thinly veiled. It engorged me and hurt my stomach. I felt bloated and sick and violently ill from the piles of junk food that I took in to fill the void. I began craving the healthy meals he used to cook for me. I started to pine for a time where I would no longer sit there alone, in my room, looking the mess I really was. I rose from the pile of take-out wreckage and surveyed my dirty hole of a bedroom. I was disgusted by myself.

Step one: Put on pants.

Step two: Make my bed.

Step three: Get on with the rest of my life. Eat a salad for dinner. Move on. Make myself a better man so that I could find a better man. I knew in my heart of hearts that I could never treat myself to another junk food romance. I had the heart of a vegan, the passion of a carnivore, and the mind of one of those trendy, gluten-free chicks.

Sweet Revenge
☆ ☆ ☆ ☆ ☆

Categories: Desserts, Wine Bars
Neighborhood: West Village

I was never a morning person until I met Him. It had a lot to do with the way he would bolt out of bed in the morning like an excited child on Christmas. I would happily roll around in bed all morning long, drifting in and out of sleep, but he always had an urge to seize the day. There was too much world out there to see, too much to do, and nothing would get done if we just lazed around. I just wanted to lay there and hold Him, but he wanted to get up and do all of the things, almost as if to say that life was too short, and if we didn't do the things then, we'd never have the chance again. Looking back, I'm glad we took mornings together. Life really is too short, and relationships are even shorter.

My West Village life with Him was a magical one. One of my many fond memories of Him was a breakfast we had together at Sweet Revenge. Even the most romantic breakfasts—those that the rest of the world would swoon at and revel in—were almost starting to become mundane. If something was so perfect all of the time, then it eventually would become commonplace. We take these things for granted when they are gone, and at the time, my red velvet waffle was perhaps a bit too dry and the juice was too pulpy. Looking back, I'd kill to relive it again.

It's easy to long for all those romantic and intimate mornings, but I had to force myself to remember the sordid truths. I remembered how I finally put a pin in our chance of ever finding a path of forgiveness: sweet revenge. It changed so quickly, and it made my head spin to think that we could go so far from waffles and kisses to revenge and pure, unadulterated spite.

After he left me, there used to be a small part of me that truly believed he'd eventually realize he had made a mistake. I don't know why I thought this; he had clearly moved on. He had found a new boyfriend within a matter of weeks, one who was much more successful and attractive than I. He had great teeth. I knew this because I had researched him like a creepy stalker. I had to tell myself that this was okay because it was something that everyone does when left by The One. I felt dirty as I cyberstalked them, and I felt no better than Him who made his entire livelihood off of being a pixelated, idealized version of himself. I was becoming my worst nightmare: I was becoming Him. Although I had once thought that was what I had wanted, it now felt dirty and wrong. I'd said it before and I would say it again: be careful what you wish for. Yet I continued to let my bitterness take me over.

I was becoming spiteful and jealous. I was filling with rage and deceit. I wanted to make Him hurt the way that he had hurt me, even though eye for an eye was never something I thought I would stoop to. I had made a promise to Him that I would never hurt Him, but as if possessed by my jealousy, I began to let that promise seem futile and dull. Just like he had promised that he would try to change for me, now I was breaking my promise. It was something I thought I would never do.

It would have been easy to play the victim and say that the downfall of our romance was completely his fault. Looking back, I realized that I was just as guilty as he. I was a scumbag, and I wanted blood as payback for the heart that he turned rogue. Even as he was courting his new love, he incessantly came calling to me. He showed up at my door after midnight and showed up drunkenly at my work trying to kiss me. All the while there was another man who he crawled into bed with at night that was not me. It broke my heart and filled me with an unexplainable rage.

I went down the rabbit hole and plotted sweet revenge. I penned his new lover a long and detailed letter about all that had transpired between Him and I. I spilled it all: the lies, the cheating, the emotional abuse, the late night visits to my door, and his sick online obsessions. It was the lowest thing I had ever done, and I hated myself for stooping to that level. I should have known that our moment in the sun was over, but for some reason I couldn't stop myself from making sure that I was ending it with my own hands.

Revenge is not sweet. It is ugly and sad. I don't know what I was thinking—to try and break his heart like he had broken mine? I was just a wounded and damaged person. Perhaps a little crazy, definitely a lot angry. In the end, it did nothing to help either of us. I didn't feel better, and he didn't want me back. I had broken my promise, and I was just as bad as he was.

I should have taken the high road. I should have just forgiven Him and let Him find love anew. It broke my heart even more to know that I had the capability of hurting the person I had once loved more than anything in my life. I knew that I had ruined the chance of ever eating waffles with Him ever again, and sweet revenge had soiled my good name, which used to be an agent of true love.

I wished that our story had never taken such an ugly turn, and I was filled with remorse for the way with which I had handled it all. Hopefully, I had learned my lesson that revenge is not sweet. It is lonely and sad and does nothing for anyone in the end. Nobody wins, and there was never to be waffles or smiles or beautiful breakfasts ever again.

Bethesda Terrace

☆ ☆ ☆ ☆ ☆

Categories: Parks, Landmarks & Historical Buildings

At times, the future seemed like a daunting and unsure thing. Like the time we waited in line at the Central Park Boathouse to board our own private rowboat to take out on the lake. From our preemptive picnic bounty, I took a slice of soppressatta and fed it to Him.

"Meat snack," he said with a smile as he happily chewed.

"That's what I'll call you," I said. "You're my meat snack." It wasn't dirty; it was cute. He was a delicious little morsel that satiated my hunger for indulgence.

"Do you think we'll be together for a long time?" he asked. We'd not really spoken of the future before then.

"I do," I said without missing a beat. "You're my best friend. And I can't imagine being happy without you."

Truth be told, I believed every word as it fell from my mouth. I believed that I would keep Him and go through the motions with Him and let Him become part of my life for better or for worse. That's back when I believed I could really handle everything that entailed.

As spring began to poke its head out from the icy grasp of winter, I knew that in a matter of weeks I would return to the Boathouse and

Bethesda Fountain and all of those other places that were the physical embodiment of everything I held sacred. I had done it every year, and there was not a place in all of New York City (or the world, for that matter) that made me happier. The lake was where I felt most like my genuine self, and as I floated along the turtle-dotted water I could paint a picture of what the best day of my life could look like. It involved cured meats and sunshine and Him.

When I took Him to the lake for the first time, I insisted on rowing. I always did. Never one to settle for less than the most grandiose of spectacles, this was where I found my true calling. Within the picturesque diorama of park life, floating beneath the backdrop of all the expensive real estate of the West Side, I felt the weight of the City melt away. It was like my body had become one big sigh, and I escaped my neurosis-ridden head for a moment and just floated. He tossed his head over the side of the boat and let his jaw hang slack, just taking in all of the sun. I took my phone from out of my pocket and put on Courtney Love, and as I placed it beneath the seat of the rowboat, the sound reverberated off the sides from all around.

We became a big, floating spectacle amidst the other boats full of kids and tourists, and I felt not at all strange to be the proud captain of the SS *Homo*, gallantly sailing the low seas with shirtless man-candy in tow and Hole screeching the angst of my troubled youth. I'd never felt like I could get away with this kind of absurdity with any of my former boyfriends. Him? He just looked at me with puppy-dog eyes and a big goofy smile and said to me, "You're so cool. I've never been with someone so cool in my life."

It was the nicest thing he'd ever said to me. I'd always wanted to be "cool," whatever that meant. Cool as in casual. Casually whatever I wanted to be. Cool as in the fact that he wouldn't judge me for liking chick rock or my dirty Converse sneakers that had holes worn in the soles or the fact that my hair was a mess (in a non-contrived way).

"I'd marry you," he said casually as he squinted at me. He just lay there on his back taking in all the sun and being rowed around like Cleopatra down the Nile. At this remark, I nearly capsized the boat. I quickly changed the subject.

All of this talk about the future made my head spin. I was on a boat, eating cured meats, with my best friend, listening to Courtney Love, and he thought I was cool enough to marry. I remember thinking to myself, *Yes. This is the best day of my entire life. I've never, ever been happier than I am in this very moment. It could be like this always. This could really be happening.*

Cut to a few months later, and I was left to wonder how it had come so far in such a short amount of time. It was as if my relationship with Him had been linked to the seasons—we bloomed in spring, thrived in summer, and by fall began to wither and . . . well . . . fall.

I wanted to pick a fight with Mother Nature. I wanted to grab her by the hair and smash her face into a pile of the dirtiest gutter snow. The whole thing just seemed unfair, even though it was just a fact of life that summer couldn't last forever. It's such a messed up notion that when we're in the midst of July, sweating buckets and soaking our tank tops, we say how much we miss the winter and being cozy by the fire. Then comes the icy hell of January and we lament the fact that we can't be on a park bench drinking iced coffee.

That day on the lake was perfect. I didn't miss the winter, and I didn't mind the summer. I had New York in the palm of my hand, and I sat on the water with the most beautiful man I'd ever seen. My best friend. My co-pilot. My boyfriend. Him.

Boat season was returning soon. I wondered if I'd return to the boats.

Chapter Seven

MY NEW YORK LOVE STORY WAS SMATTERED with undeniable nostalgia. It was full-bodied like a Barolo and as rich as ossobuco. It was also as sour as spoiled milk and as embarrassing as a drunken McDonalds binge—the kind you wake up to the next morning and cringe when you see all of the wrappers and debris you'd decimated in your stupor. Sometimes it was elegant and beautiful, and sometimes I wished it would just go away. I was sick because of it.

While floating around like a zombie in a squinty-eyed Lexapro haze, I attempted to zone out. I kept my eyes on the ground as I walked the streets, mainly only to work and back, as to not catch sight of any of those memory-triggering bombs. I was afraid to leave the house unless I absolutely had to, mostly for fear of seeing Him on the street, but truthfully for fear of not seeing Him.

I became very good at pushing it all out of my mind and relishing in sweet denial—most of the time, of course. But sometimes I would stumble upon little artifacts of our courtship that I had purposely hidden away from myself. I'd not wanted to get rid of them because I feared that I would forget all that they had meant to me; I intentionally hid them from myself to spare me the occasional sting they would cause, which pierced even the strongest of antidepressant armor. It was utterly confusing. I had to remember to force myself to forget, and I also had to forget how to remember Him.

My laptop was like a shipwreck burial ground, deep in the pitch-black depths of the Bermuda Triangle. I'd blocked out all incoming messages from Him on my email and hidden all traces of Him on Facebook. I'd cleared my browser history and promised myself to never return to Yelp again. Even so, there were times when fragments of Him showed up in ways that would catch me off guard.

One day, months after our very last conversation, I found a letter that I had written to Him after he had first broken up with me when I went to Paris. It was the breakup after Paris and before Thanksgiving— Thanksgiving, of course, being known as "The Real Breakup." Who could keep track of all of these epic and cinematic breakups? The fucker just loved to break up. And I just loved to take Him back when he would beg for my forgiveness. I was a sucker. I was played.

The letter I found was floating around in my documents folder and was simply titled "OctNotes.doc." When I opened the file, I was immediately transported back to the place and feeling I had while I was first writing it. It was one of the many letters that I had written Him around that time (first thing in the morning, every morning), but this might have been the only one that I ever *sent* that was born of that specific point in our relationship: the point where I still believed in Him.

I could bitch and moan about the rise and fall, and the end of our story that never got its happy ending, but it would make no difference. What did matter was that at one point, before it all hit the fan or the Internet or any of that bullshit . . . one thing was absolute: I missed Him.

Every morning I wake up and start to write this letter.

Each time, I eventually relent and shut my laptop and force myself into getting on with the day at hand and hopefully the rest of my life. It's become a habit, this ceremonial "beginning of the letter." Now this habit includes a banana and a protein shake—I put on my gym shorts, make a protein shake in the blender I discovered hidden in the kitchen, and almost always awaken Duncan in the process. The banana, it always manages to fit into my routine as a substitute for the cigarette I always used to have first thing in the morning. Needless to say, a lot has changed over here.

In the morning especially, I sometimes think of the little things that I want to say to you—stupid little things that at one point made up our day-to-day interaction. Like how that cactus made a sudden turn for the better and began to grow an entirely new head. Or like how I saw the Goodwill lady with the silver dreadlocks spill an entire carton of milk in line at Lifethyme the other day. Just things that happen in my day that at one point would have happened in your day, too, were you still in the picture.

It's amazing how swiftly it all changed. All of it. I stopped sleeping in weeks ago. It was my new thing. And it made everything seem different and cast in a strange and unfamiliar light—a colder and quieter morning experience than I knew possible. The morning air began to catch that telltale chill that I know all too well, and it threatened (or promised) to conjure the oncoming dread that happens every year. It's on its way, and I know there is no way around it, so I've succumbed with open arms. I pulled out all of my coats from under my bed and readied them to be worn—elements be damned.

It wasn't just the season that was changing, and perhaps that was what startled me the most. Life can be measured in seasons rather than years here in Manhattan. That being said, I've about 52 of them under my belt, and each one has had its own distinct signature. Like that one spring that I only drank iced chai tea. Or the winter that I wore leather Dolce & Gabbana gloves with silver knuckles every day. Eventually there would come that summer that I spent with you. Being that fall is now upon us, it's easier to look at it in past tense. That was a thing that happened, and it was so . . . last season. Not one to follow the logical trend, I still have those awful Dolce gloves somewhere in the nightstand beside my bed. Naturally, I keep the memory of you not far off as well. Not hidden quite so deep in my nightstand.

When you told me that we could never be together, I did what was natural to me, the same thing I always did in the past when my heart broke: radical amelioration. In times past, it was usually as easy as dying my hair or getting a new tattoo. I knew this time was going to be a lot different, and I knew it would not be as easy. So I looked within instead of making myself up and became rather shocked at what I was finding. I knew I had to completely raze my life as I knew it, as happy and familiar with it as I had been in the past. It clearly wasn't working out—for me or for anyone else. I looked at myself long and hard and became sickened with what I saw looking back at me. Suddenly it was clear why you had looked at me with the same disdain. I was a wreck. A glutton. A caffeinated Oscar Wilde with little to no care for the future.

I started with the basics. I decided to grow some balls and fully commit to fixing my body—I had to live in it, and it was beginning to feel like a dirty skin in need of molting. I quit smoking. Completely. Never again would I ever be a slave to that horrible feeling of wanting something so badly that it kills you (metaphor much?). In doing so, I had more time than I knew what to do with on my hands. Sure, at first I panicked. I told myself I would go to the gym every day instead (which I have, save one or two days). It was only a matter of days before I started to notice a difference in my body. My arms were suddenly larger, and I could feel my chest rise and fall as I descended the stairs in my building. I felt good. It felt like suddenly I could become something that I was not, or had never been before.

It was only a week before I decided to go on a date. I was so proud of the New Me, and I felt like someone else would surely like this new version of me as well. His name was Michael, and he's 34, works at Google, lives by himself in Williamsburg, and has awesome hair and cool tattoos to boot. On our first date, we couldn't decide where to go—in the City or in the Burg. It was his idea to meet in the middle of the Williamsburg Bridge for the first time and then decide which way to go from there. It was perfect. As the sun was setting, I made my way to the middle of the bridge and waited for him. The romance was so palpable that Woody Allen would have blushed.

Eventually we made our way into Manhattan (even though the coin toss told us to go to Williamsburg—fate be damned), and Michael produced a flask of Fernet and Diet Coke from his bag. The taste instantly brought me back to the first time I saw you at Von, and you cheerfully drank yours on the rocks and leaned on the bar. I hadn't had a drink in a week or so, and it instantly went to my head and made everything seem that more real. Eventually we kissed. He came over, indulged in some PG-13 making out, and eventually went home, as he had to work in the morning.

The next time I saw Michael, he was noticeably aware that perhaps I was acting a bit strange. I had explained to him on our first date over Negronis at Freeman's that I was freshly fallen out of love. He had guessed it, actually, probably because of how uncomfortable I had been in conversation that should have come with utter ease. He asked me things like "how was your weekend?" and I could only do my best and answer truthfully with "I've been having a very, very hard time." He seemed to not mind that I was on the mend. It wasn't until a later date when we were at his apartment listening to PJ Harvey and making out and drinking wine that he called me out on my shit.

I was lying atop him and running my fingers through his beard. I looked into his eyes and saw that they were looking back at me oddly—as if he could see what was playing in my mind. He could tell that something was amiss. So I pressed myself away from him and put on my new boots (I looked amazing—you should have seen me). I didn't need to elaborate when I told him that I didn't feel okay. It was all going too fast, and I didn't feel right. Eventually I told him that I wasn't ready, and that I had to go. This was, of course, after he told me that he didn't think I was ready to be seeing someone. I didn't speak to him again after I left.

I walked through Williamsburg, and it was cold. I didn't recognize myself anymore—my aching muscles, my new boots, my lack of cigarette as crutch, my new Isabel Benenato sweater, Williamsburg, the lingering smell of Michael's

Comme des Garcons cologne. It was all alien to me, and it was terrifying. I sat on the street and put my head in my hands. I had no idea where I was or where I was going. All I could think about was you. It always is.

In my headphones, I listened to the song "Exit Wounds" by Placebo. It was from their new album, and it haunted me: "In the arms of another who doesn't mean anything to you, there's nothing much to discover. Does he shake? Does he shiver as he sidles up to you like I did in my time?"

I entered a bodega, bought a pack of Camels, took them outside, and threw the entire pack in the trash. I didn't even open them. I knew I could never return to the person I used to be, no matter how easy it could be. I went home and threw things at the walls instead.

Oh—also, the laundromat on Thompson closed the other day. All of the machines have already been ripped out, and I have no idea where I am going to do my laundry now. I suppose I will have to start dropping it off and having it done across the street, which upsets me very much. It's not a monetary thing, and I love the strange little Asian man who runs it. I just can't help but think of all of the times I did laundry on Thompson, having The Best Day of My Life. Those were days that I will never, under any circumstance, be able to shake.

I can remember it clear as day how I pulled your underwear out of the dryer and held them against my face like a weird pervert. They were clean and warm and I loved them. They were yours. Your legs went into those holes, and I loved your legs. Your butt was in that seat, and I loved your butt. I remember smiling so hard that my feet took to action magically and started dancing around the dryers. You texted me, and thought I was manic or high. I was neither. I was just really, really in love.

For all the times you hurt my feelings or tried to escape or always had one foot out the door, I could not let them get in the way of the heart of the matter. The laundromat is gone and so is the summer and so are you. These are things I know to be true. But every day—every single day—I still think about the way you made me feel more alive than I've ever felt in my entire life. I have to keep telling myself that maybe it's not you I'm sad about losing, but the feeling that you gave me. I don't know how to get it back.

So I better myself. I lift heavier weights and I dress up like someone else, like the life I live is a costume. I meet and kiss new boys, and each time I do I cannot help but run away for fear of having my heart broken again.

I know it will get better eventually. I know that it always does, and hopefully I can figure out how to be happy with myself again. Or happy with someone else. But in the meanwhile I just wanted you to know that I start to write you this letter every morning when I wake up. This is actually the far-thest I have gotten yet—I usually lose momentum and get disheartened after a paragraph or so. Every morning I wake up and feel instantly panicked that you aren't there when I roll over. Every morning I wish that I could go get you coffee—just one last time. God, how I'd give anything just to get you coffee. What I'd give to have just one more glass of wine with you at French Roast and have you look at me like you used to. I'd give anything. Fuck. You melted me. You held me so close and said that you wanted to be closer than my skin and nearly crawled inside of me. I wanted it so, so badly.

Having started writing this letter so many times, I never really thought about how I would end it. My biggest fear, I suppose, was getting a letter back in return. I fear I already know exactly what it would say, so please don't say it. Especially just to hurt me. I know you have moved on. I know you think you are better off now. I know that you thought we were doomed. I know I'm not the type of man you want to be with. It's all been said a million times before, and we've run it all into the ground. So it's not even worth opening up discussion again.

Then why even bother? Why even spend so much time every goddamn morning writing letters to you that I will never even send?

Because I love you. I loved you. I will always love you. You are the most beautiful man I've ever had the pleasure of being with, and it breaks my heart that I will never have you again. I don't want you to ever doubt your decision to leave, but I do want you to know that I didn't want you to. I've always wanted you, and I always will. You changed me in ways you will never know, and even if it was at the cost of my heart, I will never regret it.

Every day I move on a little more. I'm getting over it. But I'm also taking something with me as I go. And I'll always think of you. Every day. This is never going to change. You changed me.

Today is the day that I finish this letter.

This is the day that I'm going to push "send."

I miss you.

Brooklyn Bridge

☆ ☆ ☆ ☆ ☆

Categories: Landmarks & Historical Buildings, Parks

Although I felt like it would never come, it finally did one day. I awoke and looked out my window and was greeted by clear blue skies and rays of sunlight filtering in. Perched outside of my window on my air conditioning unit was a dove bobbing its head and looking around for what I assumed was his bird wife. They came here every spring to screw on my air conditioner, and that's how I knew that spring was finally here. I smiled as I propped myself up in bed and just stared out the window overlooking sun-splashed rooftops of the West Village. As I got up to open the window and let the day in, the dove caught me out of the corner of his eye and took flight out over the city.

I hurriedly threw on clothing and made a mad dash for the streets. My heels caught the slight breeze in the air, and I almost felt like I was skipping. It was amazing to think that just a matter of days ago, I had wanted to crawl into a hole and just give up on it all. As I fluttered around the Village, I had no idea where I was going. Frankly, it didn't matter at all. All I knew was that the sun was shining and my New York was back and I finally felt like "it" was over. "It," of course, being the winter of my discontent that I thought had ruined my heart forever.

I felt like my entire body was having an epiphany, and suddenly all of the right circumstances had become aligned in order to let me break free of the shackles enslaving me. I came to as if being resuscitated from the dead by electric shock to the heart: "clear" said the phantom doctor as he pushed the electric panels to my chest. With a jump, my body lurched up from its near paralyzing rigor and gasped for air. Suddenly, I was on the Brooklyn Bridge, and I felt like I had no idea how I got there. But my eyes were suddenly open and the sun was on my skin and I could feel the lightness coming back.

Maybe all of the horrors of the winter had been but a sick nightmare. They seemed so far away, even though they had just reared their ugly heads no more than a few weeks ago. Suddenly, I didn't hate Him for all that he had done to me, nor did I hate myself for allowing it. I no longer felt married to the pain that he had made such a reality in my day to day. It was as if I had become unlocked, like all it took was the turn of a key to release me from the chains of sorrow. Sunlight was the key, and it filled me to the brim and restored my faith in humanity.

On the topic of keys, I had noticed something about the bridge that I hadn't noticed before. I had been on the Brooklyn Bridge just about a year ago, with Him, and had failed to notice all of the locks that embellished the wires running all along it. They all had names and engagements and testaments of eternal love carved into them—it was just like that bridge in Paris. It was slightly less grand-scale, but still the same concept. People from all over the world had come here, to this place, and fastened locks to represent their steadfastness in love. It was as if to say that love really did stand a chance when it was true, and it could in fact be made into something of permanence. Too many people these days saw the notion of love as being "locked" or "trapped" into something, but I knew that there was more to it than that. Love should be something that frees you and liberates you and makes you stronger—it's that permanence and strength that the lock represents. Delving further into metaphor, I wondered what the key was in this equation. What was the key to making love stay?

The hardest thing I learned that winter was that the real battle was not to love another person—that comes easy and free when it's right—but to love oneself. Through all of the madness that I had endured in my love for Him, I found it easiest not to blame or hate Him for all of his mistakes, but to take it all out on myself for not being strong enough to handle them. I realized there on the bridge that I was not made of iron, and I wasn't like one of those locks that would require heavy-duty bolt cutters to ever be removed. I was fragile, flesh and blood, and basically a blathering pile of poems and girly love songs trapped in skin. That had to be okay, because I could never be anything else. This was who I was. I was a man enraptured with love for a city and a season and a feeling, who would never be anything but.

I'd seen the bridges of Paris, the most romantic side streets of New York, and the most pristine coral sand beaches of Tahiti in my short time on this planet. I felt connected to them each in a different way at a different time. Love has many different disguises, but you know it when you see it. I was still working on it, but that was at least what I had come to know.

I was so happy that spring was back, and with it came the doves and walks on the bridge and sunlight and, most importantly, my heart.

Chapter Eight

IT BLEW MY MIND THAT the whole affair with Him had only lasted a year. Almost to the day.

It had felt like a lifetime, probably because I had spent nearly every single day with Him. In the midst of our epic breakup, he had found it necessary to tell me over and over how much he had never really loved me or never even had fun, and that our entire relationship had been one big fight. This infuriated me the most, which was probably why he said it. I knew it was a spiteful lie, but it still stung. It couldn't have been farther from the truth, yet he had managed to almost get me to believe it. We had several fights and half-hearted separations and passionate disagreements—that was the honest truth. However, these were all just a few really bad days within the course of an entire year. As stupid as it was, it was just easier for Him to see all the bad things and never the good.

This was why I knew that we would never get our happy ending: I was an optimist, believe it or not. I saw the glass half full. He wanted to take the glass and throw it against a wall.

After he left me, he began a new relationship almost immediately. Quite honestly, it didn't shock me in the slightest. This had been the reason that we had never stood a chance to begin with: his constant desire to be validated by other men. When we first tried to end our relationship over Thanksgiving, it had been because of this same innate desire of his. I had casually looked in his laptop that he left open at my house. He had been acting oddly strange and distant, and I knew from experience when something was amiss. It broke me completely to find that he had been carrying on several conversations and happenings with a handful of other men. Messages to ex-lovers, flirtations with men around the city, and graphic and explicit texts that were quite blatantly deceit. I had known since the beginning that this was something he was capable of and that I would never make an honest man out of Him. I had chosen not to believe it because my love for Him was so strong.

When confronted, he confessed to cheating on me. I didn't know how to handle it, so that was why I fled to California. I left Him there on Minetta Lane as he slunk into a ball of hysteric sobbing not because he lost me, but because he couldn't have his cake and eat it too. I couldn't believe that my ardent love wasn't enough for Him. What I came to learn was that nothing would ever be enough for Him. That was a reality he would have to take with Him for the rest of his life.

Although he had found a new lover, he came knocking at my door constantly. He would send me text messages telling me how much he missed me as he was sitting across the dinner table from his new boyfriend. He would show up drunkenly at my work and sometimes in front of my apartment late at night. It was a nonstop barrage of emotional hardship, and I didn't know how to escape it. Because I still loved Him, for some reason or another, I let it continue to happen for a while. I couldn't understand why I had thought that his constant emotional abuse was acceptable for so long. In the end, the only thing I could come up with was that love makes people actually lose their damn minds.

At long last, springtime eventually came to Manhattan. After I found myself on the Brooklyn Bridge, I could feel that my mind was clearing and I was finally starting to see things as they really were. I felt at once liberated from the shackles of winter and the shackles of Him. I no longer hated Him for finding a new lover or for all the times he had sought out new lovers while he was still with me. If anything, I felt truly sorry for Him and his inability to be happy with just one man— even if it was just me being the one man who wasn't enough for Him. Sure, maybe I wasn't the best for Him. I'd never be one of the muscle men he lusted after on Instagram or one of the scumbags he talked to on Grindr behind my back or an ex-lover who still sent Him dick pics as a friendly reminder on Facebook. I'd never be rich like the man he left me for.

I came to realize that maybe it wasn't Him that had been the downfall of our story. Maybe it was me who was asking too much of the wrong person. It was me who had wanted things that he simply did not. And what was the matter with that?

None of it mattered to me anymore. I was me, and he was Him. I had to be okay with me to finally understand that our love had been nothing more than a changing of seasons, the falling of leaves, and the snow that in the end makes the first blossoms of spring worth it all.

I think the big lesson that needed to be learned was that not every love story has a fairytale ending. No matter how much you love someone, it doesn't necessarily mean that they will love you in return. Him and I had completely different needs, and I came to understand that was okay. I needed loyalty and honesty to make me satisfied, and he needed to sow his wild oats. After all, it was his first full year in New York City. I had been there from the start to finish of it, and it was easy to see how wild that must have been for Him. He needed to find his own Manhattan just like I had when I first arrived here all wide-eyed with wonder and hope for the possibility of finding The One. It sucked that I was not the one for Him, but it finally began to make sense.

Is it possible to have someone be your soulmate if you aren't theirs? Could the stars be fickle enough to even consider letting that be a possibility? I had to brush the stars from my eyes and begin to think about my heart from a rational point of view.

I decided to stop Yelping when the spring came. I knew that it was time to stop living in the past and trying to resuscitate a love that was struggling to take its dying breath. The hardest part, however, was the thought that our seasonal love affair had finally come full circle; now was supposed to be the time where we came to our theoretical blossoming. The boats were back, and the fireflies and the ice creams.

He decided to leave New York that summer. Just as soon as he had come, he was whisked away by his lust for life that had enraptured me to begin with. Almost like a prophecy, my timeline and his met exactly in the middle. He had a new life to live, and so did I. So I came up with a plan. I had to find a way to write my happy ending, this time without Him.

I desperately waited for my *Eat, Pray, Love* moment.

My problem was that I was a stubborn son of a bitch. I thought that if I just pushed harder, loved harder, and tried harder, that it would eventually work out. Eventually, he broke up with the guy he moved on to and decided to take a summer job in the Hamptons, where he met another man who he fell immediately in love with. After the summer, he would move back to California or (as fate would have it) Paris. As he took to a new start in the Hamptons, I decided to take a new start where the heart of the matter had come from: Manhattan.

I revisited all of the places I had Yelped about as the days went on. I learned how to have breakfast at French Roast without wanting to die. The warmth of springtime led me to Sundaes and Cones for my taro root ice cream, and I looked at the famous poop cake over in the display case and just smiled. I only ordered one scoop this time, and I took it for a walk through the East Village and tried to hum a happy song. With Him gone from the island, and soon from New York entirely, I decided that I would take back the places and the things that I thought he had taken away from me.

Finally, I started to learn how to eat again. Although I still constantly craved the comfort of my signature meal at Café Mogador, I started to walk down 9th Street instead of Saint Mark's when looking to take lunch. I tried new places, and much to my surprise found that eventually I started to taste the food again. It didn't taste like sawdust anymore, and the most astounding thing that I noticed was that I actually grew to become hungry. This blew my mind.

Hunger is the strangest thing.

No one can escape it, and it's one thing in life that will always be absolute. Hunger is Desire's sister, and she knows your name and your address. Hunger can be a yearning for a person, or it can be a desire to take something new into your life. Suddenly, I felt a hunger return that I had forgotten even existed. It was the hunger in its most human and mortal form. I wanted a cheeseburger. And I wanted it so badly that my mouth began to water.

I walked with no direction and an open mind. New York City was littered with hundreds of places where one can get a mind-blowing cheeseburger, and probably a few of them hadn't ever been haunted by the ghost of my failed relationship. In my headphones, Sinead O'Connor's new song was on full blast, and I remember the words that turned my direction for the rest of my life.

I don't wanna love the way I loved before
I don't wanna love that way no more
What have I been writing love songs for?
I don't want to write 'em anymore
I don't wanna sing from where I sang before
I don't wanna sing that way no more
What have I been singing love songs for?
I don't wanna sing them anymore
I don't wanna be that girl no more
I don't wanna cry no more

I don't wanna die no more
So cut me down from this here tree
Cut the rope from off of me
Set me on the floor
I'm the only one I should adore

As I walked with the spring breeze blowing lightly on my skin, I found myself steadily gaining momentum. My walk became a stride, my gait became a jog, and suddenly I found myself running down Prince Street. I artfully dodged through the hordes of tourists and SoHo shoppers as I weaved my way into the heart of downtown.

I stopped in the middle of Broadway and watched as tourists and chic women in black dresses and businessmen in exquisitely tailored suits flocked into Dean & Deluca on the corner. Out of breath from my sudden sprint, I reached into my pocket to fish for my phone. I opened the Yelp app and typed in the word "cheeseburger." At this, I smiled.

Oh.

So that's what that's for.

I turned back from where I had just run from and didn't think twice about it. Covered in sweat and still listening to my song, I made my way to a restaurant called Little Prince for the first time. That day I had what was probably one of the best cheeseburgers of my entire life: the French Onion Soup burger, with grilled onions and Emmental cheese. I would say it was a solid five-star worthy bit of heaven.

I know he would have loved it.

I knew I'd be coming back to Little Prince often to enjoy my new spot. It made me happy to know that I didn't have to Yelp about it.

Plus, if word got out that they had New York's best burger, I'd never be able to score a table so easily. Let's keep this one to ourselves. Don't tell a soul about it.

My review for the first lunch of the rest of my life didn't need to be Yelped or screamed or whispered seductively into the ear of the most handsome man on earth. It didn't need to end in a tearful fight that made the waitress nervous. It was just me and my burger, in my city, with the memory of a love so strong that it nearly made me lose my appetite. That's not an easy thing to do, as any of my closest friends will tell you. I'm a hungry guy, and apparently I'm a professional at this kind of thing. All that needed to be said was that, at that point, everything was delicious.

And finally, I was full.

Epilogue: Yaffa Café

ANOTHER ONE BIT THE DUST.

Yaffa Café had been one of my most frequented restaurants in New York City for over a decade, and now it was just another faded memory that would be lost in the mire of my timeline. For fourteen years, I had gone to the café at odd hours of the night to sit and celebrate with the people I had come to collect in my life as a New Yorker. Holidays, birthdays, post-shift binge eating, and first dates had all had their moments in that garishly decorated room brimming with the electric and eccentric buzz that the East Village used to radiate. This place felt like my living room, and I felt as if it had watched me grow from a post-punk street urchin teenager into the man I was today.

It's that notion of progress that I've watched for years as the places I once held sacred vanished from the topography of my love affair with New York. Restaurants, for me, were the markers of my own evolution into what I was to become. Yaffa's "Open All Night" opulence and 7A's comforting kitsch were reflections of the once-whimsical heart that I grew living in downtown Manhattan at a point in history where no one was sure where our whole story was going to end. Me and her—Manhattan, that is.

We weren't the same anymore. A place like Yaffa was meant to live in a time before hashtags and selfies and Yelp reviews. It was a place that was meant to be a kind of secret—a little window into a world that existed after the bars closed and the lights went up and would still take you in and stuff you full of hummus and fill you with too much cheap Pinot Noir until you were imbued with the neon pink glow of delirium that the place forced upon your senses. In those glossy red banquettes, I had deep belly laughs with the friends I had collected here, and a good cry or two over stuff that didn't matter anymore, and kisses with boys whose names I couldn't even remember. These were my carrot-ginger flavored memories that would stay with me for the rest of my days.

I sat outside of Yaffa Café on a brisk fall day and stared at the skeleton that it had become. The lights were all off, and some of the furniture had been placed outside of the patio wrapped in cellophane. My immediate reaction was to plunder—just grab a piece of something so that I could have a physical reminder of this place that was going extinct. Like I could hold a fork or coffee mug from the place and feel as if I had a jabberwocky claw in my hand. In the end, I resisted. With a heavy heart, I turned my back and walked on Saint Mark's to Tompkins Square Park.

It had been almost a year since the world had come to a crashing halt on that horrible day in November—Thanksgiving. So much had changed, and I could barely recognize the world I once lived in, and for this I was not sure if I should be thankful. Certain parts of the city that I'd once cherished had become distant memories, and new places that I'd discovered had become illuminated in a new light. On my own, I felt like Columbus once again, discovering a brave new world; one already inhabited by natives who looked on at me puzzled and confused as to what I was doing there. Being single again was something that I had to learn anew, but I did not expect it to be as foreign a feeling as it was. As a naturally (and fiercely) independent person, I had hoped that I could swing back into my natural stride like I'd not been changed by the whole matter that had brought me to my newfound state of emotional numbness. Alas, I just moved on like any rational-minded individual would do. With new eyes and my feet on the ground, I knew it was time to start over.

I thought about California a lot around that time. I daydreamed of returning to the canyons of Malibu and hiking to peaks overlooking the ocean and foraging for prickly pears with which to make fresh margaritas for me and my family. I dreamed of being a stranger again in a foreign land not haunted by the memories of another relationship gone awry. For the first time in what seemed like forever, I began to grow weary of all the things about Manhattan that had once brought me joy. Although in my heart of hearts I loved everything about her, I felt as if I had to let go completely to understand why any of it had mattered in the first place.

Although I had hoped to write a study on falling in love, it was evident that there was a bigger lesson to learn in all of this. It's easy to fall in love in Manhattan—everyone's doing it. Movies, books, television shows, and plays have all been born of the magical spark that comes when one falls in love here. There's no doubt that it's a special place that makes the heart act like a hummingbird on crack. The real lesson that I had to learn in my years spent on this island was how to let go.

I let go of my fears and dove straight into a love that threatened to destroy me. I let go of a man who would never have the same love for me that I had for him, even though it was the hardest thing that I had ever done. I knew that it was only a matter of time before I had to let go of New York if I ever wanted to grow.

Although my love for the city was evident, it no longer posed any challenges for me. I'd conquered it, in a way. I learned every nook and cranny of the beautiful West Village, every spot from which to catch a beautiful sunset or share an intimate glass of wine with a person I adored. Every bagel I ate for breakfast, no matter how expertly crafted, tasted the same. I just wanted to fall in love again, and seeing that I was nowhere near ready to fall in love with another man, then I would have to fall in love again with a new city. I began to wonder which was more important to me: my love for someone else or my love for myself and wherever I chose to rest my head.

My relationship with him had only lasted the better part of a year, and yet my love affair with New York had lasted nearly fourteen. New York showed up when I called and never left me high and dry. It terrified me to leave, but I knew that I had to give myself another shot at finding myself and my heart. The waves were calling, and to them I would answer and give my all, just as I had with the concrete monster known as Manhattan.

I quit my job that fall and decided to go.

I gave up my apartment on Minetta that I had dreamed of living in all of my young life. I was suddenly overcome with waves of memories from when I first moved to the city and used to haunt the street that had now become my home. I recalled sitting at the long-deceased Café Esperanto on Macdougal Street, chain smoking and writing poetry in my little black journal, daydreaming of what it would be like to live in this magical place. Although it took many years to see it all come to fruition, I did one day endure long enough to see my dreams come true.

That's the funny part about seeing your dreams come true: once they do, we're foolish enough to ask for more. This is perhaps not the worst fate, and to settle for a life without wanting more could have been the death of me. Surely I could have stayed in the West Village, living, loving, and working until I became old and stagnant. It could have been a beautiful life. But I would have always wondered what could have been if I took the other road.

In the end, it all comes back to love. I wondered if I could ever love a city as much as I had loved New York, and this made me wonder if I could ever love another man as much as I had loved him. There was only one way to find out, and so I packed my bags and prepared to embark on a new love story. I'd said it before, and I knew it to be true that the best part of a love story is always the beginning—that's where all the hope is. Hope for finding The One. Hope for completing my heart. Hope for a life that was fulfilling and would not let me down in the end.

New York would always be there if I ever found I'd made the wrong decision. And should that happen, perhaps I would return there with a changed perspective—maybe moving to, I don't know, Queens or something bonkers like that, which would make my head spin. I knew that I wasn't closing any doors, only opening new ones.

I broke my promise to stop Yelping for one last trip around the block. I wrote a love letter to Yaffa Café, and the memory of a New York that was slowly fading from my view.

Breaking up is hard to do, as anyone who has ever been in love will tell you. Letting go is even harder. But if I am sure of anything from my whole affair with New York City, it is that the story is never over. It keeps going as long as you let it. Life will knock you down and let you see stars and make your heart play tricks on you. It will bring you people who will change your life and take you to dinner in places that will incite a Pavlovian response in you just by thinking of them.

Eventually the day came, and I found myself at JFK with my life crammed haphazardly into two gigantic bags. Over my shoulder, I carried an empty guitar case filled to the brim with tee shirts, and in my hand I carried my cat in his little box. I peered in to look at him—his eyes were glazed over in a drug-induced haze that the vet had prescribed him for travel. I felt the same: hazy and confused as to the road that lay ahead. He let out a timid meow.

"I know," I said to him. "I'm scared, too."

I took him into the restroom with me and set him on the counter by all the sinks. Packing myself into a tiny bathroom stall with my gigantic bag, I fished around in the front pocket of my guitar case. I pulled out the first small orange pill bottle that contained my prescription. I took a deep breath and dumped the entirety of its contents into the toilet. I did the same with the rest of my pills. They settled in the bottom of the bowl, and I flushed them down. A smile, pure and true, streaked its way across my face for the first time in what felt like forever.

The only thing left to do is let go.

Move on.

Find your love, whatever or wherever it may be.

Remember where you came from, but more importantly, where you are about to go.